ECONOMIC ISSUES, PROBLEMS AND PERSPECTIVES

FEDERAL BUDGET CONTROL: A BALANCED BUDGET AMENDMENT OR STATUTORY LIMITS?

ECONOMIC ISSUES, PROBLEMS AND PERSPECTIVES

Additional books in this series can be found on Nova's website under the Series tab.

Additional E-books in this series can be found on Nova's website under the E-book tab.

AMERICA IN THE 21ST CENTURY: POLITICAL AND ECONOMIC ISSUES

Additional books in this series can be found on Nova's website under the Series tab.

Additional E-books in this series can be found on Nova's website under the E-book tab.

ECONOMIC ISSUES, PROBLEMS AND PERSPECTIVES

FEDERAL BUDGET CONTROL: A BALANCED BUDGET AMENDMENT OR STATUTORY LIMITS?

DARREN GROFF
AND
BLAINE RUTHERFORD
EDITORS

Nova Science Publishers, Inc.
New York

For permission to use material from this book please contact us:
Telephone 631-231-7269; Fax 631-231-8175
Web Site: http://www.novapublishers.com

Library of Congress Cataloging-in-Publication Data

Federal budget control : a balanced budget amendment or statutory limits? / editors, Darren Groff and Blaine Rutherford.
p. cm.
Includes index.
ISBN 978-1-61942-051-9 (soft cover)
1. Budget--United States. 2. Government spending policy--United States. 3. Tax and expenditure limitations--United States. I. Groff, Darren. II. Rutherford, Blaine.
HJ2051.F3887 2011
352.4'80973--dc23

2011041370

Published by Nova Science Publishers, Inc. † New York

CONTENTS

PREFACE

One of the most persistent political issues facing Congress in recent decades is whether to require that the budget of the United States be in balance. Although a balanced federal budget has long been held as a political ideal, the accumulation of large deficits in recent years has heightened concern that some action to require a balance between revenues and expenditures may be necessary. The debate over a balanced budget measure actually consists of several interrelated debates. Most prominently, the arguments of proponents have focused on the economy and the possible harm resulting from consistently large deficits and a growing federal debt. Another issue involves whether such a requirement should be statutory or made part of the Constitution. This book provides an overview of the issues and options that have been raised during prior consideration of proposals for a balanced budget constitutional amendment with a focus on statutory limits on total spending as a method of budget control.

Chapter 1- One of the most persistent political issues facing Congress in recent decades is whether to require that the budget of the United States be in balance. Although a balanced federal budget has long been held as a political ideal, the accumulation of large deficits in recent years has heightened concern that some action to require a balance between revenues and expenditures may be necessary.

The debate over a balanced budget measure actually consists of several interrelated debates. Most prominently, the arguments of proponents have focused on the economy and the possible harm resulting from consistently large deficits and a growing federal debt. Another issue involves whether such a requirement should be statutory or made part of the Constitution. Some proponents of balanced budgets oppose a constitutional amendment, fearing that it would prove to be too inflexible for dealing with future circumstances.

Chapter 2- March 2, 1995 was a pivotal day in the history of our country. On that day, the U.S. Senate failed by one vote to send a balanced budget amendment to the states for ratification. The amendment had passed the House by the required 2/3rd majority previously and the Senate vote was the last legislative hurdle before ratification by the states.

If that amendment had passed, then we would not be facing the fiscal crisis we now face. If that amendment had passed, then balancing the budget would have been the norm, rather than the exception over the past 25 years and we would have nothing like the annual deficits and skyrocketing debt that we must address today.

Chapter 3- The author is an associate professor of political science at the University of Rochester and a s enior scholar at the Mercatus Center at George Mason University.[1] His research focuses on legislative politics and fiscal policy. The author has written papers and a book on the subject of budget rules, and he has been following the debate over our nation's future fiscal course with great interest.[2] In his testimony, he shows why attempts to create long-term fiscal reform, stabilize the debt, and reduce the deficit are likely to fail in the absence of Constitutional budget rules.

Chapter 4- Author Robert Greenstein, president of the Center on Budget and Policy Priorities, a policy institute that focuses both on fiscal policy and on policies affecting low- and moderate-income Americans believes, like most others who analyze fiscal policy developments and trends, that the nation's fiscal policy is on an unsustainable course. As part of the authors' work, they have been analyzing proposed changes in budget procedures for more than 20 years. The authors have conducted extensive analyses of proposals to write a balanced-budget requirement into the Constitution, among other proposals.

Chapter 5- The author is Andrew Moylan, Vice President of Government Affairs for the National Taxpayers Union (NTU), a non-partisan citizen group founded in 1969 to work for lower taxes and smaller government at all levels. NTU is America's oldest non-profit grassroots taxpayer organization, with 362,000 members nationwide. He looks forward to this hearing as the beginning, rather than the end, of robust and serious deliberation of constitutional protections for taxpayers, hopefully to include hearings by the full Committee on the Judiciary in this chamber and the Senate."

Chapter 6- Often when there is dissatisfaction with budgetary levels, budget process reforms are proposed to mandate a specific budgetary policy or fiscal objective. This report focuses specifically on one such budget process reform—the concept of creating a statutory limit on total spending.

As discussed in this report, a total spending limit consists of statutory long-term or permanent limits on federal spending coupled with a statutory enforcement mechanism that would make automatic reductions in spending in the event that compliance with the limits is not achieved through legislative action. Such spending limits would comprise any new spending as well as spending that results from previously enacted law. By encompassing all types of spending, and by including a statutory enforcement mechanism, a total spending limit attempts to remedy a perceived limitation of the congressional budget resolution, under which Congress establishes limits on spending in various categories that can be enforced or waived by Congress at its own discretion.

In: Federal Budget Control
Editors: D. Groff and B. Rutherford
ISBN: 978-1- 61942-051-9

Chapter 1

A BALANCED BUDGET CONSTITUTIONAL AMENDMENT: BACKGROUND AND CONGRESSIONAL OPTIONS

James V. Saturno and Megan Suzanne Lynch

SUMMARY

One of the most persistent political issues facing Congress in recent decades is whether to require that the budget of the United States be in balance. Although a balanced federal budget has long been held as a political ideal, the accumulation of large deficits in recent years has heightened concern that some action to require a balance between revenues and expenditures may be necessary.

The debate over a balanced budget measure actually consists of several interrelated debates. Most prominently, the arguments of proponents have focused on the economy and the possible harm resulting from consistently large deficits and a growing federal debt. Another issue involves whether such a requirement should be statutory or made part of the Constitution. Some proponents of balanced budgets oppose a constitutional amendment, fearing that it would prove to be too inflexible for dealing with future circumstances.

Opponents of a constitutional amendment often focus on the difficulties of implementing or enforcing any amendment. Their concerns have been numerous and varied. How would such a requirement affect the balance of power between the President and Congress? Between the federal courts and Congress? Although most proponents would prefer to establish a balanced budget requirement as part of the Constitution, some advocates have suggested using the untried process provided under Article V of the Constitution for a constitutional convention as an alternative to a joint resolution passed by two-thirds vote in both houses of Congress. Although the inclusion of a balanced budget amendment as part of the congressional agenda has muted this debate in recent years, proposals for a convention are still possible, and raise concerns that one might open the way to an unpredictable series of reforms. The last American constitutional convention convened in May 1787 and produced the current constitution.

These are also questions that will be raised and considered by Congress concerning the provisions that should be included in such a measure as it sifts through its options. Congress ultimately will decide whether consideration should be given to a constitutional requirement for a balanced budget; and if it decides to proceed, it will need to decide whether there should be exceptions to the requirement, or if it should include provisions such as a separate capital budget or a limitation on expenditures or revenues. For example, as reported from the House Judiciary Committee, H.J.Res. 1 in the 112th Congress includes provisions that would require a super majority to allow a budget with outlays in excess of receipts, to allow outlays to exceed 18% of the "economic output" of the United States regardless of whether the budget were balanced, to increase the debt limit, or to increase revenues. S. 365, enacted August 2, 2011 (P.L. 112-25), provides that the House and Senate vote on a balanced budget amendment between September 30, 2011, and December 31, 2011, and includes expedited procedures for its consideration.

This report provides an overview of the issues and options that have been raised during prior consideration of proposals for a balanced budget constitutional amendment

I. Introduction

The debate over the need to establish a constitutional limit on spending or debt is nearly as old as the nation itself. Thomas Jefferson is often cited as an intellectual forefather in the current debate because of his distrust of government debt. He once wrote that the way to cure what he felt was extravagant spending by the Administration of John Adams was a constitutional amendment that took away the power of the federal government to incur debt.[1] Support for such an idea has waxed and waned continuously since that time. Support was echoed in the "Contract With America" advanced by Republican House candidates during the 1994 congressional campaign, and by the wide consensus on a balanced budget as a political ideal, especially since the late 1970s. The current call for a constitutional amendment to require a balanced budget reflects its status as one of the most persistent political issues of recent decades. In the current Congress, the House Judiciary Committee has reported a proposal, H.J.Res. 1, that includes provisions that would require a super majority to allow a budget with outlays in excess of receipts, to allow outlays to exceed 18% of the "economic output" of the United States regardless of whether the budget were balanced, to increase the debt limit, or to increase revenues.

Generally the term *balanced budget* simply refers to a situation wherein the annual expenditures made by the government are equal to its receipts. Disagreement about just exactly how these key components should be defined and measured has been one of the chief stumbling blocks in the consideration of balanced budget proposals. Although these sound like straightforward concepts, this definitional problem is far from trivial; any sound definition must say what is to be included and, at least by inference, who is to be responsible for insuring that its provisions are carried out. When coupled with additional provisions, as with H.J.Res. 1, the debate takes on even greater complexity.

The Deficit as an Issue

The goal of balancing the budget was rarely controversial during the 18th and 19th centuries, and budget deficits were considered abnormalities to be tolerated only in extraordinary circumstances such as war. Prolonged deficits in the aftermath of the Civil War and the depression of 1893 had an impact on the way in which budgeting was done, but did not alter this objective. As late as the 1920s, adherence to this ideal meant congressional commitment to a policy of surpluses throughout the decade to retire some of the huge debt accumulated due to the First World War.

The unprecedented magnitude of the deficits incurred during the Great Depression of the 1930s and World War II seem a watershed in American fiscal history, but those deficits did not represent a revolution in fiscal policy. Although the New Deal and the "new economics" ascribed to John Maynard Keynes are intertwined in the minds of many, there was likely no direct and substantial influence of Keynes on President Roosevelt's fiscal policies.[2] Indeed, Keynes' *General Theory of Employment, Interest and Money*, the work that spurred the transformation of economic thought, was not published until 1936. The Roosevelt Administration's fiscal policy in the 1930s accepted deficits as a consequence of "providing relief," but not as part of a deliberate policy to bring about recovery or full employment.[3]

The transformation of economic thought that followed Keynes had a growing impact on fiscal policy after World War II, demonstrated by such legislation as the Employment Act of 1946.[4] Even President Dwight Eisenhower, who was sometimes criticized for making a "fetish" of balancing the budget,[5] had some degree of flexibility on this question. He stated that, "it has sometimes seemed a little bit odd that we have to make our whole ... economic cycle coincide with the time it takes the earth to get around the sun."[6]

By the time of the Kennedy Administration, the ideal of budget balancing had lost its primacy as an influence on fiscal decisions. Advocates of Keynesian economic theories supported the concepts of counter-cyclical spending and "full employment" budgeting. These concepts implied increased government spending and tax cuts to offset downswings of the economy even if a deficit resulted, and decreased spending, tax increases, or both in order to run surpluses during upswings. This idea was based on the premise that governments should balance the economy, not simply the budget. Although there is no generally accepted Keynesian orthodoxy, even among economists,[7] and there is much debate on the impact of government in the economy and on the economics of budget balancing.

The Call for a Balanced Budget Amendment

The declining significance of balanced budgets as the singular goal of fiscal policy prompted opposition efforts to establish formal legal underpinnings for the principle of a balanced budget. Perhaps the first example of this occurred in 1935 when Senator Millard Tydings introduced the first measure designed effectively to require the federal budget to be balanced (S.J.Res. 36, 74th Congress). This resolution unsuccessfully sought to prohibit appropriations in excess of revenues in the absence of new debt authorization, and require that any new debt be liquidated over a 15-year period.

The following year Representative Harold Knutson introduced the first proposed constitutional amendment that would have required a balanced budget (H.J.Res. 579, 74th Congress). That proposal would have allowed for the possibility of deficits, but would have established a per capita limitation on the federal public debt during peacetime. Since the limit suggested was lower than the outstanding debt at the time, it would have effectively mandated budgetary surpluses.

The first congressional action beyond the introduction and referral of proposals occurred in 1947. By special arrangement, the Senate Appropriations Committee had a balanced budget amendment jointly referred to itself as well as the Senate Judiciary Committee. The Appropriations Committee reported the measure on May 5, 1947.[8] However, the Judiciary Committee did not take any subsequent action, and no further formal consideration occurred.

Since the 1930s, dozens of proposals have been made to require a balanced budget, to limit the size or growth of the federal budget or of the public debt, or some combination of these ideas, including several notable recent efforts. These have come in the form both of bills and proposed constitutional amendments.

The Debate in Recent Decades

Possibly reinforced by previous experience that many Members of Congress have had at the state level, where balanced operating budgets commonly are required, the issue has remained alive.[9] For a period, some observers feared that the goal of a balanced budget, or even the Keynesian ideal of using budget policy to balance the economy, had been totally abandoned. This was particularly so in the 1990s because until FY1999, no President had proposed a budget in balance since FY1971.[10] Further, before FY1998, the federal government had not ended a fiscal year in surplus since FY1969 (see Appendix A). During that period the size of annual deficits had increased, both in terms of dollars and as a percentage of Gross Domestic Product (GDP). The increasing level of both the federal deficit and debt (see Table 1) increased the popularity of the idea of mandating a balanced budget.

In particular, it generated strong interest in the idea of using constitutional change as a remedy for seemingly intractable current budgetary problems. Indeed, Presidents Ronald Reagan and George H.W. Bush supported this position. President Bill Clinton also expressed support for a balanced budget, although he opposed using a constitutional amendment to require one.

Popularity for a balanced budget amendment arguably waned during the late 1990s as the budget came into balance. Between 1985 and 2002, other statutory budget controls were in effect as part of the Balanced Budget and Emergency Deficit Control Act of 1985 and the Budget Enforcement Act of 1990. Further, a combination of spending decreases, revenue increases, and a thriving economy brought the budget into balance, and a surplus existed from FY1998 through FY2001.

Table 1. Federal Surplus/Deficit and Debt: FY1969-FY2010 (billions of current dollars)

Fiscal Year	Surplus(+)/Deficit(-)	Debt Subject to Statutory Limit
1969	+3.2	356.1
1970	-2.8	372.6
1971	-23.0	398.7
1972	-23.3	427.8
1973	-14.9	458.3
1974	-6.1	475.2
1975	-53.2	534.2
1976	-88.4	621.6
1977	-53.7	700.0
1978	-59.2	772.7
1979	-40.7	827.6
1980	-73.8	908.7
1981	-79.0	998.8
1982	-128.0	1,142.9
1983	-207.8	1,378.0
1984	-185.4	1,573.0
1985	-212.3	1,823.8
1986	-221.2	2,111.0
1987	-149.7	2,336.0
1988	-155.2	2,586.9
1989	-152.6	2,829.8
1990	-221.0	3,161.2
1991	-269.2	3,569.3
1992	-290.3	3,972.6
1993	-255.1	4,315.6
1994	-203.2	4,605.3
1995	-164.0	4,884.6

Fiscal Year	Surplus(+)/Deficit(-)	Debt Subject to Statutory Limit
1996	-107.4	5,137.2
1997	-21.9	5,327.6
1998	+69.3	5,439.4
1999	+125.6	5,567.7
2000	+236.2	5,591.6
2001	+128.2	5,732.8
2002	-157.8	6,161.4
2003	-377.6	6,737.6
2004	-412.7	7,333.4
2005	-318.3	7,871.0
2006	-248.2	8,420.3
2007	-160.7	8,921.3
2008	-458.6	9,959.9
2009	-1,412.7	11,853.1
2010	-1,293	13,510.8

Source: *Historical Tables: Budget of the United States Government F2012.* Table 1.1—Summary of Receipts, Outlays, and Surpluses or Deficits: 1789-2016, and Table 7.2—Debt Subject to Statutory Limit: 1940-2015.

a. Figures combine the amounts for FY1976 and the Transition Quarter that occurred when the start of the fiscal year was shifted from July 1 to October 1.

Concern has recently spiked once again over an increasing deficit and its potential effect on the nation's fiscal and economic health. The budget deficit each year from 2009 to 2011 has been the highest ever in dollar terms, and significantly higher as a share of GDP, than at any time since World War II. Under current policies, the federal debt is projected to grow more quickly than GDP, leading observers to term it unsustainable. While there has been no difficulty financing the deficit to date, it has been argued that at some point, investors could refuse to continue to finance deficits that they believe are unsustainable.[11]

According to some observers, the deficit problem is due to a budget process that permits the government to run persistent substantial deficits and to a political system wherein deficit spending may be rewarded. The fact that responsibility for deficits cannot be indisputably assigned to any one action or actor, or even to either undertaxing or overspending alone, leaves balancing the budget as a visible, but unrealized, priority. This has meant a surge of recent support for measures guaranteeing a balanced budget, while deficits have grown to unprecedented size.

Despite fiscal and budgetary policies that doubled the national debt in the first five years of his Administration, President Ronald Reagan was an outspoken advocate of the ideal of a balanced budget. Even before the beginning of his tenure as President, during his 1980 campaign, he wrote "Excessive Federal spending and deficits have become so engrained in government today that a constitutional amendment is necessary to limit spending."[12]

In his first inaugural address, Mr. Reagan spoke against public spending that had "piled deficit upon deficit," and had "mortgag[ed] our future and our children's future for the temporary convenience of the present."[13] Later, during his second term, he spoke of an "economic bill of rights" with a balanced budget amendment as its centerpiece, and suggested that it was long overdue.[14]

In his first budget submission (FY1991) President George Bush reiterated these themes, stating that a balanced budget amendment should be adopted to "halt the steady build-up of national debt," in order to "protect the interest of future generations."[15]

President Clinton's approach was more guarded: supportive of the idea of a balanced budget, but generally opposed to a constitutional requirement. In a 1993 letter to congressional leaders, Clinton characterized the proposed constitutional amendment approach as a "budget gimmick" whose vagueness would result in "appointed judges with life tenure" making budget decisions that he felt should be made by elected lawmakers.[16] On March 16, 1994, President Clinton sent a letter to Congress in which he stated his opposition to a constitutional amendment, despite his overall support for deficit reduction.[17] This opposition was more subdued in his 1995 State of the Union Address, when he reiterated his support for deficit reduction.[18] In his 1997 State of the Union Address, however, President Clinton made his opposition to a constitutional amendment plain. Balancing the budget, he stated, did not require rewriting the Constitution. He further stated that "I believe it is unnecessary and unwise to adopt a balanced budget amendment that could cripple our country in time of crisis later on and force unwanted results such as judges halting Social Security checks or increasing taxes."[19]

During the 1994 congressional election campaign the Republican Party (as well as a number of Democratic candidates) continued to champion the cause of a balanced budget constitutional amendment. Included in the "Contract With America" signed by many Republican House candidates in 1994, and a central part of the agenda for the Republican majority elected to both Houses that year, was support for a balanced budget amendment. The version included in the "Contract With America" also incorporated a provision to require a three-fifths vote of both houses of Congress to increase revenues.

Viewing the prospect that Congress might adopt a balanced budget amendment, the Governors of a number of states urged caution in embracing specific amendment language, further complicating the debate. Many of those attending the 1994 Republican Governors' Conference, while supporting the concept of a balanced budget amendment, expressed concern that it could increase the financial burden of the states by encouraging Congress to pass laws imposing mandates and requirements without providing funding to carry them out.[20] The chairman of the National Governors' Association, Howard Dean characterized the proposal for a balanced budget amendment a "political show," and said that no state legislature "in its right mind" would approve an amendment that didn't also include safeguards against unfunded mandates.[21]

While lawmakers continued to introduce legislation proposing a balanced budget amendment, popularity waned until relatively recently. Just six months into the 112th Congress, more proposals have been introduced for a balanced budget amendment than in any Congress since the 105th. The House Judiciary Committee considered and reported H.J.Res. 1 (112th) on June 23, 2011. All 47 Senate Republicans have said they favor a balanced budget amendment.[22] Further, a Balanced Budget Amendment Caucus was founded last year by a bipartisan group of Members of Congress with a membership of over 60 Members.

On the other hand, there has also been recent objection to the idea of a balanced budget amendment. When asked in a press briefing about President Obama's support for a balanced budget amendment, Press Secretary Jay Carney stated,

> What we don't think is necessary is to amend the Constitution or to pass a across-the-board spending reduction measure that will, for example, in both cases, seriously under-fund Medicare and Social Security, and does the exact opposite in many ways of what the President has said is necessary, which is take a balanced approach to our long-term deficit and debt problems.[23]

Prominent former lawmakers from both political parties who were present during the last significant push for a balanced budget amendment, have recently voiced objection to the idea of a balanced budget amendment, particularly if its passage is coupled with legislation to increase the federal debt limit as a way to make the debt limit increase more tolerable. Former GOP appropriator and Senate Budget Chairman, Judd Gregg stated,

> Conservatives should not tolerate those who would condition their willingness to make the tough, important votes that will address our fiscal chaos on unrealistic and impractical ideas that will have no impact on the problem. They will not come to pass in time to stop the government from spending us into oblivion. It is not uncommon for representatives and senators to propose amendments to controversial legislation that have no viability. This tactic gives them the excuse to avoid the difficult votes that might actually have an impact on a critical issue. This approach is the political equivalent of "hiding in the corners." The debt ceiling is an opportunity for real action. It can be used to force immediate action to adjust the nation's present course, which is headed towards fiscal disaster.[24]

Former Democratic Senate Majority Leader Tom Daschle stated,

> I was once a supporter of a constitutional balanced budget amendment that was proposed by my friend and former colleague Sen. Paul Simon in the early 1990s. We both believed that the gravity of a constitutional requirement coupled with lawmakers' sworn fidelity to the Constitution would be powerful enough to successfully overcome this political inertia. It won't. The answer will not come with just the constitutional requirement. It comes from members of Congress who are willing to work together to find real solutions, make difficult choices and achieve real results. It has been done before and can be done again. It was not easy to reduce spending or to raise taxes, but we did it. We made the unpopular choices in 1990, 1993 and 1997.We did not try to dodge the bullet. We bit the bullet, multiple times. We made steady progress reducing the deficit beginning in 1990 and ultimately turned it into a budget surplus from 1998 through 2001. We did it without undermining the sanctity of our Constitution or degrading it to push an ideological agenda.[25]

In July of 2011, the House passed H.R. 2560, titled Cut, Cap, and Balance, which included a provision stating that the public debt limit could be raised from $14.29 trillion to $16.7 trillion, but only if Congress agreed to a balanced budget amendment. The Senate voted to table the measure by a vote of 51-46 on July 22, 2011. After extended negotiations between Congress and President Obama, a different measure to increase the public debt limit, S.365, the Budget

Control Act of 2011 (P.L.112-25), was enacted on August 2, 2011, with a provision stating that the House and Senate shall vote on a balanced budget amendment.

A balanced budget has become a central objective of many recent efforts to reform the way the federal government operates, and is mentioned as a possible benefit in others. Achieving this goal is far from a simple matter however. Despite significant support for the concept of a balanced budget amendment, the failure to achieve a two-thirds vote of approval in both houses of Congress has been a reflection of the complexity of the issue, as well as unsettled questions concerning potential difficulties involved in implementing it. Historically, public opinion studies have routinely shown broad support for a balanced budget.[26] These same polls have also indicated that a majority of those interviewed generally favors spending increases in most policy areas and reductions in taxes. These incompatible public attitudes convey to the President and Congress contradictory policy mandates.[27] Such inconsistencies augment the quandary reflected by more than 50 years of congressional consideration of a balanced budget amendment.

There have often been two almost separate debates occurring simultaneously on the subject of a balanced budget requirement: whether there should be a balanced budget and whether there should be a constitutional amendment. The pros and cons of a balanced budget may be related to the pros and cons of a constitutional requirement, but they are not identical.

II. The Constitutional Amendment Approach

Probably the most popular method advocated for ensuring that the federal budget is balanced has been a constitutional amendment. Although it would require a two-thirds vote of approval in both houses of Congress as well as ratification by three-fourths of the states before it could become effective, most of the debate has focused on the constitutional amendment approach.

Arguments of Proponents

Arguments for and against a balanced budget amendment include economic, symbolic, and political appeals. Those advanced most prominently by proponents have focused on three things:

- the morality of balanced budgets, and the impact of current deficits on future generations of taxpayers;
- the economic benefits of reducing the deficit, particularly in the form of lower interest rates, enhanced savings rates and overall economic growth; and
- the expectation of improved public attitudes towards political institutions and politicians if balanced budgets are achieved.

Proponents of a constitutional amendment also cite the failure of past statutory attempts to compel a balanced budget. In their view, a constitutional amendment would be more binding by its nature and thus act as a surer means of achieving the desired result. A constitutional amendment, unlike a statute or rule, could only be superseded by another constitutional amendment. Without this discipline, proponents believe, the goal of a balanced budget would not be attained because of the conflicting pressure to spend.

Most proposed amendments have assumed that enforcement mechanisms could be separately enacted as statutes, but that a constitutional provision would be primarily self-enforcing. For example, in a 1985 report accompanying a proposed amendment, the Senate Judiciary Committee stated that

> The Committee expects the Congress and the President to carry out their responsibilities under the proposed amendment through both (a) the authority presently available to Congress and the President to affect and influence the fiscal process; and (b) any new authority created by Congress under its Article I enforcement authority, and otherwise consistent with the Constitution by which the Congress and the President can affect and influence the fiscal process.[28]

In 1993, the Senate Judiciary Committee stated that

> Flagrant disregard of the proposed amendment's clear and simple provisions would constitute nothing less than a betrayal of the public trust. In their campaigns for reelection, elected officials who flout their responsibilities under this amendment will find that the political process will provide the ultimate enforcement mechanism.[29]

The question of judicial involvement has been a persistent concern of opponents, but advocates of a balanced budget amendment reject the argument that a constitutional amendment would provoke rampant judicial interference with federal budgeting. They suggest that most parties would lack the standing to bring suit, and that most issues arising under an amendment would not be justiciable because they would not present a case or controversy as mandated under Article III, and thus would likely be limited.[30] For example, it would appear that standing is lacking when a third-party litigant attempts to sue to contest governmental action that he claims injures him as a taxpayer. In *Frothingham* v. *Mellon* the Court denied standing to a taxpayer suing to restrain disbursements of federal money to those states that chose to participate in a program to reduce maternal and infant mortality; her claim was that Congress lacked power to appropriate funds for those purposes and that the appropriations would increase her taxes in future years in an unconstitutional manner. The Court, noting that a federal taxpayer's "interest in the moneys of the Treasury ... is comparatively minute and indeterminate" and that "the effect upon future taxation, of any payment out of the funds ... [is] remote, fluctuating and uncertain," held that plaintiffs had failed to allege the type of "direct injury" necessary to confer standing.[31] They also suggest that even if the courts did hear such cases, the political question doctrine enunciated in *Baker* v. *Carr*[32] would place most cases outside the realm of judicial resolution.

Some have also proposed that the judiciary could be limited by including specific language in an amendment that would explicitly define their role (see section on judicial review in chapter VI of this report).

Arguments of Opponents

The constitutional amendment approach is not, however, without controversy. Practical difficulties in enforcement, and the potential for judicial involvement have been among the most salient arguments of opponents.

Concern over possible judicial involvement with the power of the purse is as old as the Constitution. Alexander Hamilton in *The Federalist* (number 78) reassured his readers that the judiciary was designed to have "no influence over either the sword or the purse."[33] During previous congressional consideration of balanced budget amendments, questions of standing and judicial authority have been raised and debated, but no conclusive answers have been reached.

Despite any expectation of self-enforcement, opponents argue that such an amendment would inevitably lead to involvement by federal judges, and ultimately by the Supreme Court, in the budget making process. Indeed, this possibility was what caused Robert Bork, then a federal judge and formerly Solicitor General during the Nixon Administration, to write,

> The results of such an amendment would be hundreds, if not thousands, of lawsuits around the country, many of them on inconsistent theories and providing inconsistent results. By the time the Supreme Court straightened the whole matter out the budget in question would be at least four years out of date and lawsuits involving the next three fiscal years would be climbing toward the Supreme Court.[34]

Additionally, Senator George Mitchell stated during the debate on S.J.Res. 58 in 1982:

> Although its sponsors have expressed faith that the courts would not intervene in the budget-writing operations of the Congress, it is difficult to find any justification for that faith.... I believe that it is impossible for anyone to predict, with any degree of certainty, what the courts may do at some future time.[35]

Opponents respond to assertions that judicial involvement would be minimal by suggesting that standing to bring suit may well exist in numerous circumstances.[36] The Supreme Court has previously expressed a standard for determining standing in terms of whether the litigant has alleged injury-in-fact, that is "distinct and palpable" and not abstract, conjectural, or hypothetical, or personal injury that is "fairly traceable to the ... allegedly unlawful conduct ... likely to be redressed by the requested relief."[37] Even an inability to show standing, however, would not necessarily limit the number of suits. Numerous suits could be brought (to gain publicity, for instance) without regard to their merit.

The question of what would be precluded from judicial review is not something that can be predicted with certainty. For example, the Origination Clause of the Constitution, which mandates that all bills for raising revenue shall originate in the House of Representatives, has traditionally been regarded as a matter entirely internal to Congress, and left for the House to decide as a matter of its prerogatives. However, in *United States* v. *Munoz-Flores*,[38] the Supreme Court rejected a claim that a case based on the Origination Clause was nonjusticiable. This, and other recent cases, would seem to narrow the bounds of what is nonjusticiable.

The experience of state governments indicates that concern over judicial involvement in budgeting is realistic. In some states the judiciary has become involved with the operation of various aspects of budgeting to impose budget balancing remedies (e.g., requiring tax increases, limiting expenditures generally or preventing implementation of specific spending laws). The possibility that federal courts could invoke such remedies prompts concern about the potential such actions would have for causing a significant shift in the balance of power among the branches of the federal government.[39]

Opponents also counter the arguments of the amendment's advocates that such a requirement would result in benefit to the economy generally. Although most opponents do not argue that a smaller deficit would be inherently harmful to the economy, they do argue that mandating a balanced budget can produce harmful results. Specifically, they suggest that a balanced budget amendment would require Congress to counteract the budget's automatic countercyclical stabilizers in the event of a recession. That is, such a requirement would force the government to raise taxes or cut spending (or both) at a time when it would be most likely to have a negative impact on the economy.

Concerns an Amendment Would Need to Address

A number of difficult questions would be posed if a balanced budget amendment were adopted. These difficulties do not necessarily establish any inherent barrier to a constitutional amendment, but they do raise concerns about how an amendment would operate in practice. One of the chief concerns, and one that would affect a statutory approach as well, is the question of predictability. According to former Senator Howard Metzenbaum,

> there is a high degree of inherent uncertainty in spending and revenue projections. It is impossible to guarantee congressional budget decisions at the beginning of a fiscal year will lead to a balanced budget at the end of the year.[40]

Although some proposed amendments do not explicitly require a fiscal year to end in balance, most would measure compliance against a standard of actual outlays or receipts. Because of the sensitivity of both tax receipts and many expenditures to economic conditions, achievement of a balanced budget would be dependent upon the accuracy of predictions for performance of the economy in a given year, and not solely on congressional good faith efforts to enact budgetary legislation that would result in projected compliance.

It could also be difficult to prevent policy choices at the federal level that could have the effect of circumventing or systematically evading a balanced budget requirement. The Congressional Budget Office has suggested that this would be a real possibility, or even a probability, if the advocates of the need for a constitutional amendment are correct about a bias toward increasing federal spending.[41] Several types of actions might in effect avoid the restraints imposed by a balanced budget amendment:

- *increased use of regulatory, rather than budgetary, action.* In applicable areas this would impose costs on state or local governments or the private sector.
- *increased use of loan guarantees.* As contingent liabilities they would not necessarily be included in the budget. Current budget rules require only the projected subsidy cost of such guarantees to be recorded as a budget item.
- *increased scope for activities by Government-Sponsored Enterprises (GSEs) or other non-governmental agents.* Because a balanced budget amendment would apply only to the government, debt issued or activities undertaken by such entities would be exempt from its requirements.

An additional concern raised by people in several state governments is that a federal balanced budget requirement would cause additional burdens to fall on state governments. Congress attempted to answer this in 1995 through the Unfunded Mandates Reform Act.[42] This act generally limits the ability of the federal government to consider legislation that would impose mandates on state or local officials without providing the funds to implement them. Congress may, however, waive this prohibition. There is also some concern that if a federal balanced budget requirement caused significant cuts in federal programs, that at least some states would find it necessary to make compensatory increases in their own spending, regardless of whether such expenditures were mandated by the federal government.

These problems are not beyond remedy or substantial mitigation, but experience in the states, as well as in the federal government, suggest that they are fundamental and bear careful attention.

III. Congressional Consideration of Proposed Constitutional Amendments

For more than six decades, Congress has shown an interest in a balanced budget requirement. Because balanced budget proposals are often in the form of proposed constitutional amendments, which are under the jurisdiction of the House and Senate Judiciary Committees, these committees have been in the forefront of the debate. As indicated in Table 2 and Table 3 below, the Senate Committee on the Judiciary has conducted hearings on balanced budget amendments on at least 23 days extending back to the 84th Congress. It also reported nine joint resolutions between the 97th and 105th Congresses.[43] The House has held hearings less often, but its Members have considered balanced budget constitutional amendments on seven separate occasions: in the 97th, 101st, 102nd, 103rd, 104th, 105th and 112th Congresses. This section summarizes congressional hearings and floor action in consideration of balanced budget amendments.[44]

Table 2. Senate Judiciary Committee Hearings On Balanced Budget Amendments

Congress	Measure(s)	Date	Publication Number
84th	S.J.Res. 126, 133	June 14, 1956	printed (no doc. number)
94th	S.J.Res. 55, 93	September 23, Oct. 7, 1975	printed (no doc. number)
96th	S.J.Res. 2, 4, 5, 6, 7, 9, 10, 11, 13, 16,18, 36, 38, 45, 46, 56, 76, 79, 86, 93	March 12, May 23, July 25, Oct. 4, 11, November 1, 1979	96-41
	S.J.Res. 126	January 14,[a] Feb. 22,[b] 1980	96-67
97th	S.J.Res. 9, 43, 58	March 11, April 9, May 20, 1981	J-97-45
	S.J.Res. 58	May 29,[c] 1981	J-97-12
98th	S.J.Res. 5	December 12, 1983,[d] March 6, 1984	J-98-88 (S.Hrg. 98-1084)

Table 2. (Continued)

Congress	Measure(s)	Date	Publication Number
99th	S.J.Res. 13	May 7, 1985	J-99-22 (S.Hrg. 99-241)
100th	S.J.Res. 3, 4, 8, 11, 25, 50, 112, 161	March 23, 1988	J-100-59 (S.Hrg. 100-1076)
101st	S.J.Res. 2, 9, 12, 183	July 27, 1989	J-101-36 (S.Hrg. 101-1009)
103rd	S.J.Res. 41	March 16, 1993	J-103-4 (S.Hrg. 103-384)
	S.J.Res. 41	February 15, 16, 17, 1994	J-103-41 (S.Hrg. 103-996)
104th	S.J.Res. 1	January 5, 1995[e]	J-104-1 (S.Hrg. 104-506)
105th	S.J.Res. 1	January 17, 22, 1997[e]	J-105-1 (S.Hrg. 105-115)

Source: U.S. Senate. Committee on the Judiciary. Legislative and Executive Calendar, Final Edition, 80th-104th Congress. For the 104th Congress: U.S. Senate. *Balanced Budget Constitutional Amendment. Report to Accompany S.J.Res. 1*. S.Rept. 104-5, 104th Congress, 1st session (Washington: GPO, 1995); for the 105th Congress: *Congressional Record* (daily edition). All hearings listed conducted by the Subcommittee on the Constitution or its predecessor Subcommittee on Constitutional Amendments unless otherwise noted.

a. Field hearings conducted by the full committee in Mobile, AL.

b. Field hearings conducted by the full committee in Salt Lake City, UT.

c. Field hearings conducted in Phoenix, AZ.

d. Field hearings conducted in Los Angeles, CA.

e. Hearings conducted by the full committee.

Hearings on a Balanced Budget Amendment

In addition to the hearings held by the Senate Judiciary Committee listed in **Table 2**, there have been hearings conducted by several other committees, including

- **House Judiciary Committee**—October 15, November 17, and 18, 1987 (serial no. 85), July 10 and 11, 1990 (serial no. 143), January 9 and 10, 1995 (serial no. 5), and February 3, 1997 (serial no. 1); March 6, 2003 (serial no.1); May 13, 2011 (not yet printed);

- **House Budget Committee**—April 28, May 6, 11, 12, 13, and 19, and June 3, 1992 (serial nos. 102-42 and 102-43), and February 5, 1997 (not printed);
- **Senate Budget Committee**—June 4 and 10, 1992 (S.Hrg. 102-693);
- **Senate Appropriations Committee**—February 15, 16, 17, and 18, 1994 (S.Hrg. 103-423);
- **Joint Economic Committee**—September 11, 1984 (S.Hrg. 98-1260), January 20 and 23, and February 16, 1995 (S.Hrg. 104-74, parts 1, 2, and 3 respectively).

Besides the hearings conducted by these committees on balanced budget proposals, a number of other hearings on budget process reform generally have touched upon balanced budget initiatives.

Floor Consideration of Amendment Proposals

Between 1981 and 1997, the Senate Judiciary Committee has approved nine balanced budget proposals and reported them to the full Senate (see Table 3). Five of these measures were considered on the Senate floor, one in each of the 97th, 99th, 103rd, 104th, and 105th Congresses. Additionally, in the House proposed constitutional amendments to require a balanced federal budget have advanced to floor consideration without committee support on four occasions, in the 97th, 101st, 102nd, and 103rd Congresses. The House Judiciary Committee also reported a proposed amendment that was considered on the floor in the 104th Congress. The first floor consideration was in 1982 when both the Senate and House debated such measures. The House Judiciary recently reported a proposed amendment on January 23, 2011, which has not yet been considered on the House floor.

97th Congress

In the Senate, consideration of S.J.Res. 58 during the 97th Congress produced the first approval of such a measure when the Senate adopted the resolution 69-31 on August 4, 1982, following 11 days of floor deliberation.[45] Later that year, following a successful discharge petition effort led by Representatives Barber Conable and Ed Jenkins, the House considered a similar proposal. H.J.Res. 350 was considered under the terms of a king-of-the-hill rule[46] (H.Res. 604) on October 1, 1982. A substitute offered by Representative Bill Alexander that would have required the President to submit a balanced budget, and for Congress to adopt a statement of receipts and outlays in which "total outlays are no greater than total receipts", but not require the year to end with the budget actually balanced was defeated 77-346[47] prior to the vote on final passage. Although the measure was approved by a majority, the vote provided less than the necessary two-thirds, and the effort for a balanced budget amendment failed, 236-187.[48]

99th Congress

During the 99th Congress, the Senate Judiciary Committee reported two proposed balanced budget amendments for consideration on the floor. One of these measures, S.J.Res. 13, also included tax limitation provisions. It was placed on the Senate Legislative Calendar under General Orders, but it did not receive further consideration. The second proposal, S.J.Res. 225, was debated extensively over eight days. On March 25, 1986, the Senate rejected S.J.Res. 225, failing to achieve the necessary two-thirds majority by a single vote, 66-34.[49]

Table 3. Joint Resolutions Proposing Balanced Budget Amendments Reported by the Senate Judiciary Committee

Congress	Measure(s)	Date	Report No.
97th	S.J.Res. 58	July 10, 1981	S.Rept. 97-151
98th	S.J.Res. 5	September 20, 1984	S.Rept. 98-628
99th	S.J.Res. 13	October 23, 1985	S.Rept. 99-162
	S.J.Res. 225	October 23, 1985	S.Rept. 99-163
101st	S.J.Res. 183	July 25, 1990	S.Rept. 101-391
102nd	S.J.Res. 18	July 9, 1991	S.Rept. 102-103
103rd	S.J.Res. 41	October 21. 1993	S.Rept. 103-163
104th	S.J.Res. 1	January 24, 1995	S.Rept. 104-5
105th	S.J.Res. 1	February 3, 1997	S.Rept. 105-3

Source: For 97th-103rd Congresses: U.S. Senate. Committee on the Judiciary. Legislative and Executive Calendar, Final Edition, 97th-103rd Congress. For 104th Congress: U.S. Senate. *Balanced Budget Constitutional Amendment. Report to Accompany S.J.Res. 1*. S.Rept. 104-5, 104th Congress, 1st session (Washington: GPO, 1995). For 105th Congress: U.S. Senate. *Balanced Budget Constitutional Amendment. Report to Accompany S.J.Res. 1*. S.Rept. 105-3, 105th Congress, 1st session (Washington: GPO, 1997).

101st Congress

In 1990, again following a successful discharge effort, this time led by Representative Charles Stenholm, the House considered a balanced budget amendment. Like its predecessor, H.J.Res. 268 was considered under the terms of a king-of-the-hill rule (H.Res. 434) on July 17, 1990. A substitute with a tax growth limitation provision offered by Representative Joe Barton was rejected 184-244,[50] but a modified version of the measure offered by Representative Charles Stenholm was adopted as a substitute, 276-152,[51] before the vote on final passage. However, the measure failed to achieve the necessary two-thirds majority, 279-150,[52] and was defeated.

102nd Congress

Two House proposals in the 102nd Congress calling for a balanced budget constitutional amendment gathered over 100 cosponsors (H.J.Res. 290 introduced by Representative Charles Stenholm, and H.J.Res. 248 introduced by Representative Joe Barton). In response to the increased possibility that the House would consider a balanced budget measure, the House Budget Committee began a series of six days of hearings on the subject of a balanced budget on April 29, 1992. The hearings continued on May 6, 11, 12, 13, and 19. On May 20, 1992 a petition was filed to discharge the Rules Committee from further consideration of H.Res. 450, a special rule to extract H.J.Res. 290 from further consideration by the House Judiciary Committee and provide for its consideration by the House. The petition received the requisite 218 signatures the same day and was entered on the Discharge Calendar. A unanimous consent agreement was reached on June 4, 1992, to allow the resolution to be called up for consideration on June 10, under the same terms as if discharged, but modifying its provisions to increase general debate time on the proposed amendment to nine hours.

After agreeing to H.Res. 450, debate on the proposed amendment was begun on June 10. On June 11, the House considered a series of substitutes under a king-of-the-hill procedure. A substitute version offered by Representative Jon Kyl included provisions to limit expenditures to 19% of GNP and to grant item veto authority to the President, but was defeated, 170-258.[53] A second substitute, offered by Representative Joe Barton, consisted of the text of H.J.Res. 248 and included a provision to limit the rate of growth of federal taxes to the rate of growth of national income. It was defeated, 200-227.[54] The third substitute, offered by Representative Richard Gephardt, consisted of the text of H.J.Res. 496 and included a provision to exempt the Social Security trust fund from the provisions of the amendment. It was defeated, 103-327.[55] The final substitute was offered by Representative Charles Stenholm as a minor modification of the original text of H.J.Res. 290. It was agreed to 279-153;[56] however, the measure then failed to achieve the necessary two-thirds majority for final passage, 280-153,[57] and was defeated.

Senate consideration in the 102nd Congress was complex, but likewise did not result in passage of a balanced budget constitutional amendment. The Judiciary Committee reported a measure (S.J.Res. 18) on July 9, 1991, with an amendment (S.Rept. 102-103). This proposal gained heightened significance when the Senate adopted an amendment to the FY1993 Budget Resolution (H.Con.Res. 287) proposed by Senator Don Nickles on April 9, 1992. The Nickles amendment expressed the sense of the Senate that it should adopt a balanced budget amendment on or before June 5. The Senate agreed to an amendment to the Nickles amendment, offered by Senator Robert Byrd, which added that a balanced budget amendment should included a requirement that the President submit a balanced budget. On May 21, 1992, the House and Senate reached final agreement on H.Con.Res. 287. The resolution retained a modified version of the Nickles amendment in Section 14, expressing the sense of the Senate that it should vote by July 2 on a balanced budget amendment that included a requirement that the President submit a balanced budget, but that any amendment should be drafted or amended so as not to exacerbate any economic recession. In addition, the Senate Budget Committee held hearings on the subject of a balanced budget amendment on June 4 and 10, 1992.

After the House rejected H.J.Res. 290, Senator Paul Simon, the chief sponsor of S.J.Res. 18, announced that he would defer attempting to bring the proposed amendment to the floor of the Senate until the 103rd Congress. However, a group of Senators, led by Senators Phil Gramm, Don Nickles, and John Seymour, endeavored to keep the issue on the agenda in the Senate. On June 24, 1992, Senator Seymour (for Senator Nickles) offered an amendment to an unrelated bill (S. 2733, concerning regulation of Government Sponsored Enterprises) that would strike that measure's language and substitute the text of a balanced budget constitutional amendment. An amendment offered by Senator Robert Kasten that would have added a tax limitation provision was rejected, 33-63, on June 30.[58] Senator Robert Byrd offered an amendment to replace the constitutional requirement in the Seymour amendment with a statutory requirement that the President submit a balanced budget proposal by September 2. This amendment, as amended by a second degree amendment also offered by Senator Byrd, was rejected on June 30, 39-57.[59] After declining to amend the language of the proposed constitutional amendment, however, supporters failed by the same 56-39 margin on both June 30 and July 1 to gather the 60 votes necessary to invoke cloture in the face of a threatened filibuster, and the amendment was withdrawn on July 1.

103rd Congress

In the 103rd Congress, a balanced budget constitutional amendment was once again a significant issue on the agenda of both the House and Senate. The Senate Judiciary Committee reported S.J.Res. 41 on October 21, 1993, and the Senate began consideration of the measure on February 22, 1994, under the terms of a unanimous consent agreement. Consideration continued on February 23, and on February 24 a further unanimous consent agreement provided for Senator Simon to modify S.J.Res. 41 by incorporating language proposed by Senator John Danforth limiting the authority of the judiciary to enforce a balanced budget amendment, as well as allowing Senator Harry Reid to offer a substitute amendment. Senator Reid's amendment would have exempted Social Security and capital expenditures from the balanced budget requirement, and provided for its suspension in times of economic recession. Consideration continued on February 25, and 28, and March 1. The Senate voted first on the Reid substitute, which failed, 22-78,[60] and then on S.J.Res. 41, as modified, which failed to achieve the necessary two-thirds majority, 63-37.[61]

Meanwhile, in the House proponents of a balanced budget amendment let it be known that they would use the discharge procedure, if necessary, as they had in the past, to bring the issue to the floor. On February 24, 1994, a petition was filed to discharge the Rules Committee from further consideration of H.Res. 331, a resolution to extract H.J.Res. 103 from the Judiciary Committee and provide for its consideration. It received the requisite 218 signatures that same day, and was placed on the Discharge Calendar. Despite the failure of a balanced budget amendment in the Senate, on March 11 the House agreed to a unanimous consent request to allow H.Res. 331 to be called up on March 16 under the same terms and conditions as would govern its consideration under the discharge rule, but modifying its provisions to decrease general debate time on the proposed amendment to six hours.

On March 16, 1994, the House approved H.Res. 331 by a vote of 387-22, making it in order to consider H.J.Res. 103 as well as a series of substitute proposals under a king-of-the-hill rule. A substitute proposed by Representative Kyl, which would have limited federal outlays to 19% of GNP and provided for Presidential item veto authority, was subsequently rejected in Committee of the Whole, 179-242.[62] On March 17, the House also rejected in

Committee of the Whole a proposed substitute offered by Representative Robert Wise that would have provided a separate capital budget and exempted Social Security, by a vote of 111-318.[63] Earlier that same day, the Committee of the Whole rejected a substitute proposed by Representative Barton that would have limited the growth of federal revenues as well as required a balanced budget, by a vote of 213-215.[64] Because the votes of the Delegates and the Resident Commissioner had been decisive in the outcome, the vote was taken again in the House pursuant to Rule XXIII and the amendment was this time adopted, 211-204.[65] This substitute was later superseded, however, when the Committee of the Whole agreed by voice vote to a final substitute offered by Representative Stenholm that would have moved back the effective date of H.Res. 103 to 2001 or two years after ratification. As thus amended, H.J.Res. 103 was voted on in the House but failed to achieve the necessary two-thirds majority, 271-153.[66]

104th Congress

In the 104th Congress, the new Republican majority leadership in the House placed a balanced budget constitutional amendment on the agenda as part of its "Contract With America." On January 4, 1995, Representative Joe Barton (and others) introduced H.J.Res. 1, a proposed balanced budget constitutional amendment with a tax limitation provision. Following two days of hearings, the House Judiciary Committee reported the measure with amendments on January 11 (H.Rept. 104-3). On January 24, the House Rules Committee reported H.Res. 44 (H.Rept. 104-4) providing consideration for H.J.Res. 1 as well as H.Con.Res. 17, outlining an understanding concerning the treatment of Social Security under any balanced budget constitutional amendment. After adopting H.Res. 44 on January 25, the House took up H.Con.Res. 17, a measure that its chief sponsor, Representative Michael Flanagan, described as requiring Congress to "leave the Federal Old Age and Survivors Insurance trust fund and the Federal Disability trust fund alone when it is forced to comply with the balanced budget amendment." H.Con.Res. 17 was adopted by a vote of 412-18.[67]

In addition to H.J.Res. 1, H.Res. 44 made in order consideration of six substitutes for it. These amendments were selected from 44 amendments inserted in the *Congressional Record* between on January 13 and 20, pursuant to a notice issued by the House Rules Committee on January 11. Unlike previous years, these substitutes were not considered under a king-of-the-hill rule. Instead, H.Res. 44 provided that the House would consider and vote on each of the alternatives, and the one that received the most votes would be considered as the one that was finally adopted.[68]

After completing general debate on January 25, the House considered each of the six substitutes on the following day.

- A substitute offered by Representative Barton, identical to the version approved by the Judiciary Committee, which required a three-fifths vote to increase tax revenues. This version was adopted, 253-171.[69]
- A substitute offered by Representative Major Owens that provided for the waiver of the Article when the national unemployment rate exceeds 4%, and deleted the requirement for a three-fifths vote to increase revenues. This version was rejected, 64-363.[70]
- A substitute offered by Representative Robert Wise that would have placed capital investments in physical infrastructure and Social Security transactions off budget, and required the operating budget to be balanced. In addition, this version did not include special vote requirements for approval of a deficit or increases in the debt limit or taxes. It was rejected 138-291.[71]
- An amendment offered by Representative John Conyers that would have placed Social Security transactions off budget and required congressional action on a budget plan detailing how a balanced budget would be achieved before the Article could take effect. It was rejected 112-317.[72]
- A substitute sponsored by Representative Richard Gephardt and offered by Representative David Bonior (D-MI) would have placed Social Security transactions off budget and required an absolute majority of the membership in each House of Congress for approval of a deficit. This version also deleted any special vote requirements for increases in the debt limit or taxes. It was rejected 135-296.[73]
- The final substitute, offered by Representative Dan Schaefer, was similar to the version reported by the House Judiciary Committee (and offered as an amendment by Representative Barton) except that it required a majority of the membership of each House to approve a measure to increase revenues rather than a super-majority. It was approved 293-139.[74]

Approval of the Schaefer substitute superseded the prior approval of the Barton substitute because it had more affirmative votes. As thus amended,

H.J.Res. 1 was adopted by the House 300-132, becoming the first proposed balanced budget constitutional amendment to be approved in the House.[75]

According to news reports, following the successful passage of H.J.Res. 1 in the House, several Democratic Senators voiced concern about passage in the Senate without also producing a detailed plan for deficit reduction. A letter sent to Majority Leader Robert Dole to that effect was signed by 42 Democratic Senators.[76]

The Senate had already begun to address some of the issues raised during House consideration prior to formal consideration of a balanced budget amendment. In particular, the subject of the treatment of Social Security under a balanced budget constitutional amendment was debated during consideration of S. 1, the Unfunded Mandates Reform Act.[77]

The Senate version of the balanced budget amendment, S.J.Res. 1, was introduced by Majority Leader Dole and others on January 4 and referred to the Senate Judiciary Committee. The committee held one day of hearings on January 5 and then reported S.J.Res. 1 without amendment on January 23 (S.Rept. 104-5). On January 27, the Senate agreed by unanimous consent to begin consideration of H.J.Res. 1 the following Monday, January 30. The Senate considered the proposal for four days (January 30, 31, February 1, 2) before the first amendments were offered.

On Friday, February 3, the so-called "right-to-know" amendment was offered by Senator Daschle. It would have required that a blueprint be established showing how the deficit would be reduced and eliminated prior to the proposed constitutional amendment becoming effective. After debating the amendment on February 3, 6, and 7, the Senate voted on February 8 to table a motion by Senator Daschle to commit H.J.Res. 1 to the Judiciary Committee with instructions that the Daschle amendment (231) be incorporated into the resolution and reported back. The Daschle motion and amendment were effectively killed when the motion to table was agreed to by the Senate, 56-44.[78]

The second major issue to be addressed by the Senate was the budgetary status and treatment of Social Security under a balanced budget amendment. The issue was formally raised when Senator Reid offered an amendment on February 8 to exclude the receipts and outlays of Social Security from a balanced budget requirement. The Reid amendment (236) was debated on February 8, 9, 10, 13, and 14, before being tabled by the Senate, 57-41.[79] Previously, the Senate had agreed by voice vote to a motion by Majority Leader Dole to commit the measure to the Budget Committee with instructions that the Committee report back the resolution forthwith, and to report to the

Senate as soon as possible a plan for achieving a balanced budget without affecting Social Security receipts or payments. A Dole amendment to that motion (238) that established its final language was agreed to, 87-10.[80]

After the Reid amendment was disposed of, the Senate considered and rejected several other amendments on February 14 and 15. On February 16, the Senate voted on a motion entered by Majority Leader Dole to invoke cloture and limit further consideration of the resolution. That motion failed to achieve the necessary three-fifths majority, 57-42.[81] Later that same day, however, the Senate did agree by unanimous consent to limit further consideration and provide for a final vote on the measure on February 28.[82] In addition, two cloture votes scheduled for February 22 were vitiated. Consideration of amendments and motions to refer with instructions continued on February 22, 23, 24, 27 and 28. On February 28 the Senate agreed to an amendment offered by Senator Nunn. The Nunn amendment (300, as modified) added language limiting judicial authority to interpret or enforce the proposed constitutional amendment to situations specifically authorized by law. The provision was agreed to, 92-8.[83] After finishing consideration of all amendments and motions, the Senate recessed on February 28 and March 1 without taking a final vote on adopting the proposed constitutional amendment. On March 2 the Senate fell short of achieving the necessary two-thirds majority, 65-35.[84] Majority Leader Dole changed his vote to the prevailing side (against the amendment) for the final tally in order to take advantage of Senate Rule XIII and enter a motion to reconsider the vote at a later time.

On June 4, 1996, the Senate agreed by unanimous consent to the motion to reconsider its earlier vote. After debating the proposal on June 5 and 6, H.J.Res. 1 again failed to achieve the necessary two-thirds majority 64-35.[85]

105th Congress

On January 17, 1997, the Senate Judiciary Committee held a hearing addressing the balanced budget constitutional amendment issue. Four days later, on January 21, Senator Orrin G. Hatch introduced S.J.Res. 1, a proposed amendment to the Constitution to require a balanced budget beginning with FY2002. A second hearing was held on January 22 and the measure was reported without amendment on January 30 (S.Rept. 105-3). Six amendments, including two substitutes, were offered during the Committee's deliberations, but all were rejected.

On February 4, a unanimous consent agreement was propounded to begin consideration of S.J.Res. 1 on the Senate floor beginning the following day.

On February 5, the Senate began debate on the measure and began consideration of amendments on February 6. As in the 104th Congress, the issue of the budgetary treatment of Social Security proved to be pivotal, and no fewer than three of the amendments considered would have excluded it from the amendment's provisions. Other issues raised included allowing waivers of the amendment's provisions for national emergencies other than actual armed conflict (such as economic emergencies or natural disasters), and provision for excluding a capital budget from the amendment's requirements. In all, 15 amendments (plus one motion to refer with instructions) were considered during deliberation on the floor, but all were rejected, tabled, or withdrawn.

On February 27, a unanimous consent agreement was reached to provide for a final vote on March 4. On that day, the measure was defeated by a vote of 66-34, having failed to achieve the necessary two-thirds.[86]

A House companion measure, H.J.Res. 1, was considered by the House Judiciary Committee at a hearing on February 3. The committee began a markup of the measure on February 5 but recessed without reaching any conclusion. Also on February 5, the House Budget Committee held a hearing on the issue of a balanced budget amendment.

108th Congress

In February of 2003, H.J.Res. 22 was introduced by Representative Earnest J. Istook with 133 cosponsors. It was referred to the House Committee on the Judiciary and then to the Subcommittee on the Constitution. On March 6, 2003, the subcommittee held a hearing and on May 1, 2003, a subcommittee mark-up was held and the measure was subsequently forwarded to the full committee by a vote of 5-3. On September 22, 2004, the full committee considered the measure, but it was not reported to the House.

112th Congress

In January of 2011, Representative Bob Goodlatte introduced H.J.Res. 1, which was referred to the House Committee on the Judiciary and then to the Subcommittee on the Constitution. On May 13, the subcommittee held one day of hearings on proposed amendments to the Constitution to control the federal budget deficit. On June 15, a full committee mark-up was held and the committee voted to report the bill with an amendment by a vote of 20-12. As reported by the committee, H.J.Res. 1 includes provisions that would require a super majority to allow a budget with outlays in excess of receipts, to allow outlays to exceed 18% of the "economic output" of the United States regardless of whether the budget were balanced, to increase the debt limit, or to increase revenues.

On July 19, 2011, the House passed (by a vote of 234-190) H.R. 2560, titled Cut, Cap, and Balance. Although the bill itself was not a balanced budget amendment, it included a provision stating that the public debt limit could be raised from $14.29 trillion to $16.7 trillion only if Congress agreed to a balanced budget amendment. Specifically, it stated that the Secretary of the Treasury could not exercise additional borrowing authority as specified elsewhere in the measure, until one of the following joint resolutions were agreed to by Congress and submitted to the states for ratification: H.J.Res. 1, S.J.Res. 10, H.J.Res. 56, or another balanced budget amendment that "requires that total outlays not exceed total receipts, that contains a spending limitation as a percentage of GDP, and requires that tax increases be approved by a two-thirds vote" in each chamber. The Senate voted to table the measure by a vote of 51-46 on July 22, 2011.

After extended negotiations between Congress and President Obama, a different bill to increase the public debt limit, S. 365, the Budget Control Act of 2011 (P.L. 112-25), was enacted on August 2, 2011. Title II of the bill states that the House and Senate shall vote on passage of a "Joint resolution proposing a balanced budget amendment to the Constitution of the Untied States" between September 20, 2011, and December 31, 2011. Title II also includes expedited procedures for House and Senate consideration of the balanced budget amendment.

IV. A Constitutional Convention

Article V of the Constitution describes two methods by which the Constitution can be changed.[87] To date, constitutional amendments have always been proposed to the states by congressional action, but Article V of Constitution also provides that "on the application of two-thirds of the several states Congress shall call a convention for proposing amendments." Because this method for proposing a constitutional amendment is untried, there are many unanswered questions about such a convention.[88] A convention would not have the power to amend the Constitution directly, only to propose an amendment, and any proposed amendment would subsequently need to be ratified by three-fourths of the states in the same manner as an amendment proposed by Congress.

Between the mid-1970s and early 1980s, various interest groups lobbied state legislatures to petition Congress to call a constitutional convention to propose an amendment to limit the power of the federal government to incur budget deficits. The National Taxpayers Union and the National Tax Limitation Committee, for example, were active in these efforts to lobby for the proposal in the state legislatures. A number of other groups, including Citizens to Protect the Constitution (formerly known as Citizens for the Constitution), the Committee to Preserve the Constitution, and People for the Constitution, have been active in their opposition to a convention.

These petitions have typically requested that Congress convene a constitutional convention for the purpose of considering a balanced budget amendment and proposing it to the states for ratification. Frequently such requests have sought a convention for the "specific and exclusive" purpose of considering a balanced budget amendment, although some constitutional scholars suggest that the work of a constitutional convention could not be limited to specific subjects.[89] As a consequence, some opposition to a constitutional convention is based on concern regarding the scope of other possible amendments that might also be proposed for ratification as well as opposition to a balanced budget amendment in particular.

Other related questions have been raised regarding state applications or petitions for a constitutional convention. Some of these include (1) whether there is a specific procedure that states must follow for enacting and submitting petitions, (2) whether all the petitions must be in the same form, and (3) whether they must all be contemporaneous.[90] The Senate has on two occasions passed constitutional convention procedures bills, in 1971 (S. 215, 92nd Congress, S.Rept. 92-336), and 1973 (S. 1272, 93rd Congress, S.Rept. 93-293). Neither bill was considered in the House. The Senate Judiciary Committee also reported a bill in 1985 (S. 40, 99th Congress, S.Rept. 99-135), but it was not considered further. Although the House has not considered a similar measure, the Subcommittee on Civil and Constitutional Rights of the House Judiciary Committee held hearings on the issue in 1985.[91]

In 1983, at the beginning of the 100th Congress, 32 of the required 34 states had passed resolutions requesting a constitutional convention for proposing a balanced budget amendment. In addition to those states listed in Table 4, at least four states (California, Illinois, Kentucky, and Montana) had adopted resolutions requesting that Congress propose a deficit spending amendment, but had not asked for a constitutional convention to do so. By the end of the 100th Congress, however, two states had rescinded their applications for a constitutional convention, at least in part due to the influence of the Balanced Budget and Emergency Deficit Control Act in late 1985. Coupled with the possibility that other states would follow suit, this made the prospect of such a convention less imminent. Left unresolved, however, was the legal standing of rescissions, and the question of whether or not a state has the power to rescind such an application once it has been made.[92]

Although Alabama and Florida were the only states to rescind their applications for a constitutional convention in the 100th Congress, similar measures were subsequently passed in Nevada (1989), Louisiana (1991), Colorado (1992), Oregon (1999), Idaho (2000), Utah, (2001), North Dakota (2001) Wyoming (2001), Arizona (2003) and Georgia (2004).[93]

Table 4. States That Have Petitioned Congress for a Constitutional Convention to Propose a Balanced Budget Amendment

State	Year	State	Year
Alabama[a]	1976, 1975	Nebraska	1976
Alaska	1982	Nevada[a]	1979, 1977
Arizona[a]	1979, 1977	New Hampshire	1979
Arkansas	1979	New Mexico	1976
Colorado	1978	North Carolina	1979
Delaware	1975	North Dakota[a]	1975
Florida[a]	1976	Oklahoma	1976
Georgia[a]	1976	Oregon[a]	1977
Idaho[a]	1979	Pennsylvania	1976
Indiana	1979, 1957	South Carolina	1978, 1976
Iowa	1979	South Dakota	1979
Kansas	1978	Tennessee	1977
Louisiana[a]	1979, 1978, 1975	Texas	1978, 1977
Maryland	1975	Utah[a]	1979
Mississippi	1975	Virginia	1976, 1975, 1973
Missouri	1983	Wyoming[a]	1977, 1961

Source: U.S. Library of Congress. Congressional Research Service. *State Applications for a Constitutional Convention to Propose a Balanced Budget Amendment: Analysis and Legislative History*. CRS Report by David Huckabee. (Washington, 1984). p. 26, 27. Updated as applicable.

a. These states have rescinded their applications for a constitutional convention.

V. The Statutory Approach

An alternative for regulating the government's spending and taxing policies is the enactment of a statute requiring a balanced budget. Proponents of a statutory approach argue that it would be more flexible than a constitutional amendment, since the law itself could be modified more easily by enacting amendments to deal with changing circumstances. Advocates also argue that it could become effective quickly, in contrast to a constitutional amendment that would require a lengthy and ultimately uncertain ratification process.

Significant opposition to the statutory approach has come from those who consider it a poor substitute for a constitutional amendment. These critics contend that the adoption of a law offers no binding constraint on the actions of future Congresses; in their view the very flexibility of the approach destroys its utility. They argue that Congress can always waive or reject the rules of a previous Congress, or can overturn or supersede a statute. Critics offer the past decade's experience with attempts to mandate balanced budgets by statutory means as evidence that the political context makes circumvention virtually certain.

Previous Legislation

There have been many attempts to employ a statutory approach. The first such example is the amendment proposed by Senator Harry F. Byrd, Jr., in 1978, which became Section 7 of P.L. 95-435, a measure otherwise dealing with U.S. participation in the International Monetary Fund. The amendment stated simply that, "Beginning with fiscal year 1981, the total budget outlays of the federal government shall not exceed its receipts."[94] With almost no debate the amendment was adopted by the Senate by a vote of 58-28.[95] Without any mechanism for enforcement this commitment proved to be ineffectual, and FY1981 ended with a deficit of $79 billion. Subsequent modifications of this law have changed it from a specific commitment for FY1981 to a general affirmation of balanced budgets as a goal.[96]

A similar provision was included in P.L. 96-5, a measure to provide an increase in the debt limit. Like the Byrd amendment, the law was superseded by subsequent legislation.

Late in the 98th Congress, the House considered H.R. 6300, a bill to require the President to submit a balanced budget proposal or, alternately, to explain the reasons why one would be inappropriate. Although the measure passed under suspension of the rules, 411-11,[97] support was qualified for the measure's statutory approach because, as Representative Barber Conable said, "Until we elevate this issue to a constitutional level and create a procedure whereby this Congress will have to face up to its fiscal responsibilities, things are not going to change."[98] Because the Congress adjourned shortly thereafter, the Senate did not consider this proposal on the floor.

Table 5. Deficit Targets as Provided by the Balanced Budget and Emergency Deficit Control Act of 1985 and 1987 Reaffirmation (amounts in billions of dollars)

Fiscal Year	Original Target	1987 Revision	Actual Deficit
1986	171.9		221.2
1987	144		149.8
1988	108	144	155.2
1989	72	136	152.5
1990	36	100	221.2
1991	0	64	269.4
1992		28	290.4
1993		0	255.0

Source: For original target amounts: P.L. 99-177, 99 *Stat.* 1038-1101; for revised target amounts: P.L. 100-119, 101 *Stat.* 754-784; for actual amounts: *Budget of the United States Government FY2012. Historical Tables.* Table 1.1—Summary of Receipts, Outlays, and Surpluses or Deficits: 1789-2016.

After it failed to achieve the two-thirds vote necessary for a constitutional amendment in 1990, the House considered H.R. 5258, a bill to require the President to submit a balanced budget to Congress each year, for the Budget Committees to report, and for Congress to consider, a budget resolution that was balanced. However, it did not require Congress to adopt a budget resolution in balance, nor did it require the fiscal year to end in balance. This measure was criticized by some as less than a serious attempt to attain balance and one that would merely provide "one more set of rules to waive."[99] Nevertheless, a majority of the House agreed with Representative Leon Panetta who said that the measure would require the President and Congress to "lay out in specific terms how ... to [achieve] a balanced budget" rather than simply establish a balanced budget as a general goal.[100] After a vote to recommit the bill to the Government Operations Committee with instructions that it hold hearings on its implications failed 181-244, the bill was passed by a vote of 282-144.[101] The Senate took no subsequent action on the measure.

Gramm-Rudman-Hollings

The most prominent attempt by Congress in to use the statutory approach as a means of achieving a balanced budget was the Balanced Budget and Emergency Deficit Control Act of 1985 (also known as the Gramm-Rudman-Hollings Act) and its 1987 Reaffirmation.[102] At the heart of this law was a timetable with mandated annual reductions in budget deficits intended to produce a balanced budget.

In addition to the specific deficit targets included in the text of the law, the act differed from the earlier Byrd amendment because it included a specific enforcement mechanism. Based on the assumption that institutional forces made it difficult, if not impossible, to achieve a balanced budget, the new law established the sequestration process. This process required the President to issue an order canceling budget authority to reduce the projected deficit to the level mandated by law. Although the original automatic sequestration mechanism was struck down by the Supreme Court in *Bowsher* v. *Synar*,[103] the 1985 law contained a fallback procedure that, lacking the automatic provision, was felt to be inadequate by Congress. The subsequent enactment of an amendment to the law in 1987 reinstated a modified procedure for an automatic trigger for the sequestration process and reaffirmed the desire of Congress to come to grips with the budget deficit.

The act was amended, and effectively supplanted, in 1990 by the Budget Enforcement Act of 1990 (P.L. 101-508, 104 *Stat.* 1388-573 through 1388-630). These changes shifted the focus of congressional budgetary control from achieving a specific deficit target to limiting congressional actions that would increase the deficit.[104] The new Act retained a series of deficit targets, but these targets would be adjusted for changing economic and other conditions rather than fixed as they had been under the 1985 and 1987 Acts. The 1990 Act established deficit targets through FY1995, but these did not require or project a balanced budget at that time. In 1993, the enforcement provisions of the Budget Enforcement Act were extended through FY1998 (P.L. 103-66, 107 *Stat.* 683-685), and in 1997, the enforcement provisions were extended through 2002 (P.L. 105-33) but again a balanced budget was not required.

VI. Analysis of Typical Provisions of Proposed Balanced Budget Amendments

What follows is a general discussion of language commonly used in proposals for a balanced budget amendment. In particular, the discussion addresses provisions that have been included in balanced budget proposals, and how some of these provisions could be subject to varying interpretations. Many of the points addressed in this analysis have been raised during previous consideration of balanced budget amendments, particularly on the floor of the House in 1982, 1990, 1992, 1994, and 1995, and in the Senate in 1982, 1986, 1994, 1995, and 1997.

A number of these interpretations might have achieved some measure of consensus among Members of Congress concerning their general meaning. However, no determinative judgments have yet been made on the vast majority of the issues discussed here, and parts of a proposed amendments' language may well be subject to interpretation. Especially in the absence of any extensive legislative history, these unresolved issues would presumably need to be treated by statute, or interpreted by the courts, or both. Because it would be by its nature new to the federal government with far reaching consequences, even in its most basic form, a balanced budget amendment would raise some questions concerning its meaning and enforcement.

All of the proposed amendments have as their central purpose a limitation on the budgetary freedom of Congress, although they pursue this objective in a number of different ways. Each of the measures proposes to require a balanced budget, but they display great variety regarding how to achieve this end and about the nature of the budgetary process and the roles that should be played in it by the President and Congress.

Use of Estimates

In their most direct form, balanced budget proposals require that "total outlays shall not exceed total receipts for a fiscal year." This is most often coupled with a proviso to allow an excess of outlays if they are approved by a vote of three-fifths in each chamber. Most proposals, either explicitly or implicitly, would allow any enforcing or implementing legislation to be based on estimates, but these would generally not supersede the requirement that actual balance at the end of a fiscal year be measured in absolute terms.

A common alternative approach would permit estimates to be used to measure compliance with the amendment's requirements. One common formulation of this is to require that Congress adopt a statement of receipts and outlays prior to a fiscal year, in which total outlays are not greater than total receipts. This is sometimes coupled with a provision that "Congress and the President shall ensure that actual outlays do not exceed the outlays set forth in such statement." This type of amendment would thus not require that at the end of the fiscal year the budget be in balance. Actual outlays could not exceed projected outlays, but the relation between projected and actual receipts is not explicitly addressed. Receipts less than the projected level would produce a deficit, but not be a violation of this type of amendment language.

Using estimates to measure compliance could also be applied to both outlays and receipts. This approach would prohibit estimated outlays from exceeding estimated receipts, but not prohibit end of the year actual outlays from exceeding end of the year actual receipts. In one form that has previously been introduced this would simply require a two-thirds vote to approve a budget resolution that recommends an excess of outlays. Because the amounts in budget resolutions are projections, such a proposal would not impose any requirement for actual end-of-year balances. Such an approach is not inconsistent with the practices of some states. According to a General Accounting Office report (now called the Government Accountability Office), at least nine states with balanced budget requirements do not require a year-end balance, and several others allow a deficit to be carried over to the next fiscal year if necessary.[105]

The reliability of estimates is crucial, especially in cases where the proposed amendment would require adherence to a standard of balance based on actual outlays rather than projected outlays. Under a variety of circumstances either the President, or Congress, or both would have an incentive to skew estimates of receipts in the same or opposite directions. If one branch favored spending cuts, it would have an incentive to estimate receipts at a relatively lower level (and thus restrain spending). Alternately, if one branch favored relatively higher spending, it would have an incentive to estimate receipts at a correspondingly higher level. These incentives could have profound implications for enforcement.

The prohibition on excess outlays in the absence of a three-fifths vote would in most cases be absolute and require adjustments to compensate for inaccurate estimates of outlays. The inability to estimate accurately the outlays that will result from entitlements is demonstrated with regularity. In recent years, supplemental appropriations have been necessary to cover the mandatory outlays associated with such programs as veterans' benefits and agricultural subsidies. There are a number of open questions about the impact of this type of provision on mandatory spending, especially that which is provided in annual appropriations and supplemental appropriations acts. Would it have the effect of requiring supplemental appropriations to achieve three-fifths support in each chamber to provide necessary funds for entitlement programs? Would it require three-fifths support to allow the release of funds already appropriated but not yet converted to outlays? If spending must be cut or deferred to keep actual outlays in balance with receipts during a fiscal year, how would such restrictions be applied to entitlements? Would this amendment implicitly establish a constitutional power to delay outlays for entitlements, or even to cancel such payments?

Some proposals, while considered as proposed balanced budget amendments, would not actually prohibit deficit spending. For example, they could simply require that either the President's budget or Congress' concurrent budget resolution be balanced, but not necessarily bar appropriations or outlays in excess of revenues. Another possibility would mandate that the budget be balanced only with respect to expected revenues or outlays so that an economic downturn that decreased revenues and increased outlays would not put the government in violation of the Constitution. These proposals could pose problems because they contain an obvious incentive favoring "rosy" forecasting of the economy and of revenues. Many proposals also provide that the requirement for balance could be waived in certain circumstances. Various proposals allow for these waivers in the case of a national emergency, low economic growth, a declaration of war or by congressional passage of a resolution by a super-majority, such as three-fifths or two-thirds.

Conversely, some proposals seek to prohibit Congress from making appropriations in excess of anticipated revenues for a fiscal year. These could be narrowly construed so that, to the extent that deficits result from actions other than those taken by Congress in the appropriations process itself, the amendment would not be an obstacle to deficits. If this interpretation were to prevail, the executive departments might be permitted to spend in excess of revenues, provided they had the budget authority to do so.[106]

Super-Majority Requirements

The requirement for a super-majority to approve a "specific excess" of outlays over receipts, while seemingly straightforward, could present issues in implementation. It could simply apply to a concurrent or joint resolution encompassing the entire budget, but there are other possibilities. Because no mechanism is provided for identifying the "specific excess" it is not clear what this means. Conceivably it could be applied to either the amount of money, to the recipient program or agency, or to both. It is unsettled how the provision would be applied in four different scenarios that could arise.

- Could the requirement be applied so that each specific program or agency would need to have a separate three-fifths majority to receive a specific amount of funds in excess of the overall ceiling?
- Could the three-fifths requirement be applied to a specific total to fund program shortfalls, which could subsequently be distributed through some mechanism that did not require a further three-fifths vote?
- Could the three-fifths requirement be applied to the release of funds for mandatory spending programs or interest on the debt in circumstances where outlays threaten to exceed receipts *after* all budgetary legislation has been enacted?
- Could the requirement be applied to a *specific program or agency* rather than a specific dollar amount, so that the agency or program could later receive some unspecified amount of funding above the outlay ceiling?

This ambiguity might give the majority party in either chamber of Congress, through their power to control the legislative agenda, power to subject the programs least popular with its leadership to the super-majority threshold. Considering such programs as separate matters could increase the likelihood of their being unfunded or discontinued. Conversely, the application of this requirement could also allow the majority leadership to circumvent the amendment and ensure deficit spending, excluding the most popular programs from any balanced budget regimen. Some programs might be popular enough to secure funding regardless of the deficit. If such programs were left unfunded until the ceiling was reached, they could then be funded subject to the requirement that they have three-fifths support in each chamber. Such a provision also leaves it unclear of the claims of mandatory outlays, including interest on the debt, in relation to other outlays in the absence of a balanced budget or a super-majority waiver.

Presidential Responsibility

More basic questions regarding the ultimate responsibility for maintaining a balanced budget are raised by proposals that establish the seemingly simple mandate that "total outlays of Government funds during any fiscal year shall not exceed the total revenue of the Government." Since outlays (that is, the actual expenditure of funds) are primarily an executive function, such language could be interpreted as a qualification on presidential spending powers, but not on Congress's ability to appropriate funds in excess of revenues. If the President's spending powers were thus the primary focus for enforcement, how would this be accomplished? Would it be necessary to statutorily increase presidential rescission or deferral powers? More significantly, would an amendment assigning responsibility to the President, either solely or jointly with Congress, to "ensure that outlays not exceed receipts" imply enhanced impoundment authority? This possibility suggests that any workable constitutional prohibition on deficit spending take into account the workings of the federal budget process and expenditure practices, as well as the division of responsibility between the executive and legislative branches.

Most measures requiring a balanced budget also include a requirement that the President submit a proposed budget with total outlays not in excess of total receipts. In addition to the requirement that his budget proposal balance estimated outlays and receipts, such a provision would also effectively make the President's role in the budget process a part of the Constitution. The President's formal involvement in the budget process currently has a statutory, rather than constitutional, basis. It stems from the Budget and Accounting Act of 1921 (codified at 31 U.S.C. 1105(a)). Historically, the budget-making process has been the constitutional preserve of Congress, requiring only the President's concurrence or passage over his veto.

Although such presidential requirements are generally included in proposals as a way to preserve symmetry between the executive and legislative branches, this is not precisely the same requirement that Congress would have to adhere to. Because of the timing of the President's budget submission[107], the estimates of receipts and outlays used in this proposal would not necessarily be the same as those used by Congress. This could mean that the President would be able to use a unilateral estimate to fashion his proposal, while Congress might have to base its spending actions on an estimate more agreeable to both branches. Also, the President's proposal would have to balance estimated outlays against estimated receipts, while under most proposed amendments Congress would ultimately have to balance actual outlays against actual receipts. This distinction is likely to revive a problem highlighted during the Reagan Administration and especially under the Balanced Budget and Emergency Deficit Reduction Act. Differing estimates and projections of the economy and the budget by Congress and the President could make it difficult to achieve budgetary goals.

Coverage and Exemptions

A concern addressed in many proposals is the issue of coverage. Lengthy debates on which activities or agencies (if any) should be exempted from the effects of sequestration under the Balanced Budget and Emergency Deficit Control Act have amply demonstrated the difficulty in reaching agreement on the issue, as well as the problems associated with exempting certain activities.

Off-Budget Activities

It is not clear whether the term "off-budget" would continue to have any meaning if a balanced budget proposal were added to the Constitution. Would the federal government be able to exclude specific entities from its presentation of the budget? Would an amendment have the effect of nullifying the current off-budget status of the Postal Service and Social Security? If the terms "all receipts" and "all outlays" used in many such proposals removed the option to create off-budget entities, it would also remove the option to consider such entities without regard to their impact on the remainder of the budget. The debate on the budgetary status of Social Security, for example, would become moot, and surplus Social Security receipts would constitutionally be treated in the same way as other government receipts as they are today. Conversely, if federal agencies or programs could be excluded from the amendment's coverage by statute, it might open a channel for manipulating the scope of the "budget" to insure that it was balanced.

Various proposals have sought to anticipate problems that could be brought about by attempts at circumvention, and have either included or excluded a variety of specific expenses or activities. These have sought to exempt such things as net interest on the public debt, Social Security, or federal credit programs. Other measures would be coupled with a capital budget, which would separate federal expenditures into one budget for current operating expenses and a second one for net investment in assets that have a useful life of several years. Even so, the question of what would be included or excluded would have to be addressed. Generally, the more inclusive the coverage, the more restrictive will be any constitutional limitation (although the reverse is true for the case of Social Security during the period from now until about 2010).

In contrast to the experiences of states, most proposals at the federal level are planned as inclusive. They are almost always defined as applying to "all receipts of the United States Government except those derived from borrowing" and "all outlays of the United States Government except those for repayment of debt principal." State governments are typically required to balance their operating, or general fund, budget, but other major fund groups (such as capital, enterprise, trust, and other special funds) may not necessarily be required to balance on an annual basis.[108]

The Senate Judiciary Committee's 1993 report accompanying S.J.Res. 41 expressed the intent of the Committee that "total receipts" and "total outlays" include "all moneys received by the Treasury of the United States, either directly or indirectly through Federal or quasi-Federal agencies created under the authority of acts of Congress."[109] The report further stated that some programs, such as the electric power program of the Tennessee Valley Authority (TVA), are not intended to be covered by this definition. The only explanation given is that the program is self-financing. It is unclear to what extent this interpretation by the Judiciary Committee would be binding. If it were, it could potentially allow the federal government to follow the state example and create other special authorities that would not be covered by the amendment's definitions of outlays and receipts.

In 1995, one of the chief sources of public opposition to a balanced budget amendment was the status of Social Security funds. Proposals to exclude the receipts and outlays of the Social Security Trust Funds (specifically the Federal Old-Age and Survivors Insurance Trust Fund and the Federal Disability Insurance Trust Fund) from the requirement for a balanced budget were among the chief topics for debate. Supporters of such an exemption argued that because Social Security operates with funds that are counted separate from the general fund of the federal government, and currently operates at a surplus, it should not be subjected to potential benefit reductions resulting from a deficit in the general fund. Further, they argue, because the accumulated surplus of the Social Security Trust Funds is held in the form of government securities, under a balanced budget amendment redemption of these securities, and thus any expenditure of these funds, would effectively require a budgetary surplus. Opponents counter that removing such a massive portion of federal transactions, whatever the source, from the discipline of a balanced budget amendment would undercut the amendment's effectiveness. In addition, they believe that an exemption for a specific trust fund could establish a channel for broad circumvention of an amendment, because it would not necessarily limit the activities that could be encompassed within the trust fund's budget.

Non-Budgetary Activities

Government-Sponsored Enterprises (GSEs) are not now considered to be a part of the federal government, and their transactions are considered to be non-budgetary rather than off-budget. These are entities established and chartered by the federal government and typically act as financial intermediaries to influence the allocation of credit in large sectors of the economy. Examples include the Student Loan Marketing Association, the Federal National Mortgage Association, and the Federal Home Loan Mortgage Corporation. They are not included in the federal budget totals because they are classified as private, although most derive special benefits from their sponsorship by the federal government. Their budgetary treatment and the range of their activities are not specifically addressed in the language or legislative history of balanced budget amendments, and it may well be assumed that they would not be included.

Waivers

The most common exception to the requirement for a balanced budget is a waiver in cases of declared war. Some proposals would also allow a waiver for military emergencies declared by law. Other provisions in proposed amendments would trigger exemptions or allow waivers. A proposal considered by the Senate in 1994 would have suspended the requirement for a balanced budget for any fiscal year, and the following fiscal year as well, if the Congressional Budget Office (CBO) estimates that real economic growth has been or will be less than one percent for two consecutive quarters during the period of those two fiscal years. Other proposals would allow a waiver of the balanced budget requirement for any fiscal year in which a declaration of national emergency were in effect. With the term "national emergency" left undefined, such a provision might well be applicable to economic as well as military emergencies. It should be noted that the duration of such a national emergency, or how its end should be determined, is left unstated.

Debt

An issue closely related to balanced budgets is federal debt and the debt limit.[110] Indeed, a number of proposed balanced budget amendments have included provisions that would make it more difficult to increase the public debt of the United States by requiring a super majority in each House to enact legislation to do so. The apparent intent is to reinforce the balanced budget requirement by making it difficult for the amount of federal debt to be increased. Without the authority to borrow funds, the government could not operate with a deficit. Indeed, some proposals deal only with debt and require a balanced budget solely by implication. At least one proposal made in the House would go further and require surpluses in order to pay down the debt.

Of particular importance is the debt to be included in such a limitation. Some proposals would apply a limitation to increases in the debt "held by the public." Others would apply the limitation to the gross public debt (e.g., all federal government debt including that held by the government's own trust funds). Another approach has been to apply a limitation to public debt with certain specified exceptions, such as for trust funds or debt for capital expenditures. These are more than minor semantic differences, and such provisions could affect aspects of federal finances beyond the balance of the annual budget. H.J.Res. 1 in the 112th Congress would require a super majority of three-fifths to increase the limit on the debt held by the public.

As defined in current law and practice, the debt subject to statutory limit includes more than just the debt held by the public. Debt held by the public involves only money borrowed by the Treasury from the public, including domestic and foreign individuals and institutions. The debt subject to statutory limit, however, includes both the debt held by the public and debt held by the federal government (or intragovernmental debt). Intragovernmental debt includes primarily debt held by trust funds.

Debt held by the public represents a financial claim by the public on the federal government in the form of bonds and other debt instruments, and is the measure of debt used in most economic analyses. The intragovernmental debt held by trust funds does not result in borrowing from world credit markets or represent a direct financial claim of the public on the government. A trust fund program itself may entitle recipients to claim present or future program benefits, and securities are held by the funds as a reserve against future benefits in excess of receipts expected in the future, but beneficiaries do not have any direct claim on the accumulated debt held by trust funds.

An increase in trust fund holdings also increases the reported gross public debt of the federal government. Generally such an increase is generated when receipts into trust funds exceed payments. Excess trust fund receipts are invested in federal government debt instruments. The portion of the gross public debt held by trust funds or other intragovernmental accounts in 2010 was approximately 33%.[111]

The distinction between gross public debt and debt held by the public could have significant implications, particularly with regard to the budgetary status of Social Security. Because it is currently accumulating a surplus for future use, the Social Security trust funds increase the amount of gross debt. Accordingly, a balanced budget amendment that requires a three-fifths vote in order to increase the gross public debt could mean that a super-majority was necessary to allow the surplus held by a trust fund to increase. Even in cases where the trust fund was in balance, the accumulation of interest on outstanding debt held by the trust fund could itself have the effect of requiring an increase in the gross public debt. On the other hand, a balanced budget amendment requiring action to increase the amount of "publically held federal debt" could make it difficult for Social Security to liquidate its accumulated reserves to pay benefits after about 2020.

Distinctions between classes of federal debt could cause the federal government to operate with separate statutory debt limits for intra-governmental debt (requiring only a majority vote for increases) and for debt held by the public.

The division of federal debt instruments into a number of different classes to secure technical compliance with an amendment could have wider implications as well. Such a phenomenon would be roughly analogous to state experience, where different debt instruments, including some not backed by the "full faith and credit" of the government,[112] are routinely issued and separately rated by financial markets.

By many accounts, state experience suggests that constitutional limitations on debt have been less than wholly effective. State legislatures have devised a wide variety of financing techniques to comply technically with constitutional limitations on the issuance of debt, including special fund financing, creation of public authorities and lease arrangements.[113] It is not implausible that the federal government would have occasion to resort to one or more of these devices if limits were placed on its issuance of new debt.

Tax or Expenditure Limitations

Another broad category of proposals includes those that place a limit on the ability of the federal government to tax or spend. Some would hold total outlays to a set percentage of some economic indicator, such as Gross Domestic Product (GDP) or Gross National Product (GNP), while others would limit increases in spending to a percentage of the growth of a particular economic indicator. Support for such provisions is derived from two chief premises: (1) the part played by the federal government in the economy has grown too large in recent decades, and (2) efforts to balance the budget should be biased in favor of spending cuts rather than tax increases. H.J.Res. 1 in the 112th Congress, for example, would limit the level of outlays to 18% of the "economic output" of the United States, regardless of whether the budget is balanced, unless there were a two-thirds super majority to support the increase.

One significant question is how a provision to limit increases in revenues might be interpreted. The term "revenue" appears in the Constitution, in this context, in Article I, section 7, the so-called origination clause. As interpreted by the Supreme Court, the phrase "all bills raising revenue" has typically meant measures raising revenue to support government generally, but not those that raise funds to support a specific governmental program.[114] This constitutional understanding of the term "revenue" therefore may differ from that used, for example, in relation to the jurisdiction of congressional committees or under budgetary statutes (such as the Congressional Budget Act of 1974). Also it could restrict the application of a tax limitation to measures that affect money raised for the general fund of the federal government, but exclude funds raised for specific programs. Another potential difficulty with the definition of revenue is that not all receipts to the federal government are currently treated equally in the budget process. Collections from the public based on the government's exercise of its sovereign powers are treated as revenues (e.g., personal income taxes). Collections by the government as a result of business-type or market oriented activities are generally treated as offsets to outlays (e.g., various royalties and licensing fees). Offsetting collections can be applied either to the outlays of a specific agency or program or to the government generally. Without further direction, through more explicit language in a proposed amendment, it is unclear how it might be interpreted.

Conversely, the phrase "increasing revenue" as used in these proposals could be interpreted to apply these requirements broadly to a wide variety of measures. Such a provision might apply not only to measures that would increase revenues by increasing the rate of taxation, but also to those that would increase revenues by lowering the rate of taxation while increasing either the taxable base or the volume of taxable activity, or both. This interpretation could have an impact on a large portion of the legislation considered by Congress. Indeed, any legislation that has the direct or indirect, effect of stimulating economic (hence taxable) activity and thereby increasing revenues might be covered by a tax limitation provision. One example of increasing revenues by increasing taxable activity would be a reduction in the tax rate on capital gains income. Although estimates differ sharply as to the longer-term effect of reducing the capital gains tax rate, the short-term effect is generally projected to increase revenues as a result of increased realization of capital gains.

It is not clear whether a limitation on increasing revenues could also be applied to measures, such as an excise tax on tobacco products, which increase tax rates to a level intended to inhibit a taxable activity. The intended effect in such a case would be a reduction in revenues, due to the inhibitory effect, rather than an increase in revenues due to the higher rate. The question remains as to whether the provision would be interpreted such that the intended effect would exempt such a measure from the restrictions of a tax limitation provision or such that the increased rate would be sufficient to place the measure in contravention of the provision.

Typically, these provisions would limit the rate of increase in revenues to "the rate of increase in national income in the second prior fiscal year, unless a three-fifths majority of the whole number of each House of Congress shall have passed a bill directed solely to approving specific additional receipts and such bill has become law." This form of limitation is the most common in recent proposals. Variations have previously been considered in both the Senate and the House.

National income (or any other measure or index) is dependent on a meaning defined either in a statute or in practice. Proponents argue that such a provision would preserve the current ratio of federal revenues to the economy as a whole. Detractors of this approach suggest that the definition of any index would be subject to manipulation, and tax policies would thus hinge on who controlled the definition. For example, in 1980 the Commerce Department revised the definition of national income to include most forms of overseas earnings, resulting in a significant increase in national income. In this case, the action taken did not directly affect the size of the economy, but did have a significant impact on the calculation of national income. Under a formula limitation, such actions could make it permissible to increase revenues regardless of the state of the economy.

In theory, this type of provision could require the government to reduce taxes if revenues were to increase at a rate faster than the economy because of changing economic conditions. For example, inflation in the late 1970s caused personal incomes to increase at a greater rate than the economy as a whole. This resulted in increased federal revenues due to higher income taxes ("bracket creep"). Although the income tax rate structure is now indexed for inflation, its progressive structure means that increases in personal income due to economic growth can still result in revenues increasing at a more rapid rate than the economy. Such a provision could also require a tax cut following a recession because of an associated downturn in national income.

More importantly, there is a two year lag between when change in national income is measured and when fiscal policy is enacted. This delay could force the federal government to adopt a counter-productive fiscal policy.

Another approach would require that measures to increase revenues be passed by a super-majority of three-fifths or two-thirds of the total membership of each House. This would allow increases in taxes beyond the rate of growth of national income, but only under one of two circumstances. First, tax revenues could increase under existing tax laws as a result of economic upturns. Alternately, they could increase as a result of any new law, if it were passed by super-majority. This type of tax limitation was endorsed in the "Contract with America" signed by many Republican candidates for the House of Representatives during the 1994 congressional election. H.J.Res. 1 in the 112th Congress includes such a provision to require a two-thirds super majority.

Alternately, some proposals might limit taxes indirectly by limiting the level of expenditures. While this method would not actually prohibit the federal government from taking action to increase revenues, it would inhibit such increases by removing the primary incentive for doing so. Even in the 19th century, the federal government did not historically operate with a sustained budgetary surplus, and it seems unlikely that a mandatory balanced budget would create an incentive to do so.[115] If expenditures were limited, any increases in revenues beyond the level necessary for balance could be applied only towards repayment of debt principal. Because the repayment of debt principal, and particularly its scheduling, is dependent on the terms under which such funds were originally borrowed, it seems unlikely that this would provide a significant incentive for the federal government to operate at a sustained surplus. Without such an incentive, the indirect effect of an expenditure limit would be to limit taxation.

Table 6. Federal Outlays and Receipts as a Percentage of GDP

Fiscal Year	Outlays as a Percentage of GDP	Receipts as a Percentage of GDP
1950	15.6	14.4
1960	17.8	17.8
1970	19.3	19.0
1980	21.7	19.0
1990	21.9	18.0
2000	18.2	20.6
2010	23.8	14.9

Source: *Budget of the United States Government, FY2012. Historical Tables*, Table 1.2—Summary of Receipts, Outlays, and Surpluses or Deficits as Percentages of GDP: 1930-2016.

The levels of the expenditure limits commonly associated with such proposals generally has been in the range of 18% to 20% of Gross Domestic Product. However, as shown in Table 6, the current level of expenditures is higher than that. Therefore, such a limitation would require significant cuts in spending as well as an overall balance of expenditures and revenues.

In any form, a limitation on revenues or outlays could create a bias in favor of tax expenditures.[116] Because in most cases these are receipts foregone by the government, rather than actual outlays, they would likely be largely exempt from any limitations on spending. Proposals to limit the growth or level of federal taxation would also favor tax expenditures over outlays. Although increasing receipts and reducing outlays are budgetarily equivalent, a limitation on increases in receipts would limit Congress's ability to eliminate tax expenditures to achieve a balanced budget. This is because eliminating tax expenditures would increase receipts rather than reduce outlays, and thus increase the risk of running afoul of such a limitation.

Judicial Review

Although H.J.Res. 1 in the 112th Congress does not include such a provision, when the Senate considered a balanced budget amendment during the 103rd Congress, the issue of judicial review was prominently debated. In particular, the Senate considered a provision to establish that the power of "any court to order relief pursuant to any case or controversy arising under this article shall not extend to ordering any remedies other than declaratory judgment or such remedies as are specifically authorized in implementing legislation." Such a provision would leave the judiciary with the authority to issue decisions concerning the meaning of the amendment or any implementing legislation, but judicial remedies of violations could only be ordered in circumstances specifically provided by law. Although such declaratory judgments[117] would be binding, courts would lack the enforcement remedies of injunctive relief or writs of mandamus. Enforcement would be left to the elected branches unless the Courts were specifically provided with authority to use these or other remedies. Limiting the judiciary to declaratory judgments might not be an entirely empty authority, but its effectiveness would depend on the parties involved respecting and following the terms of the judgment. Such a limitation on judicial remedies would represent a significant shift in the balance of power among the three branches of the federal government, and a departure from the accepted practice that allows courts to interpret constitutional disputes and determine the appropriate remedy.[118]

APPENDIX A. COMPARISON OF DEFICIT PROJECTED IN PRESIDENTIAL BUDGET SUBMISSIONS AND ACTUAL AMOUNTS, FY1965-FY2010

Table A-1. Comparison of Deficit Projected in Presidential Budget Submissions and Actual Amounts, FY1965-FY2010 (billions of current dollars)

President	Fiscal Year	Projected Surplus (+)/Deficit(-)[a]	Actual Surplus(+)/ Deficit(-)[a]
Lyndon B. Johnson	1965	-2.9	-0.2
	1966	-3.9	-0.5
	1967	+0.5	1.1
	1968	-4.3	-3.0
	1969	+8.0	+3.2
Richard M. Nixon	1970	+3.4	2.8
	1971	+1.3	23.0
	1972	-11.6	-23.4

Table A-1. (Continued)

President	Fiscal Year	Projected Surplus (+)/Deficit(-)[a]	Actual Surplus(+)/ Deficit(-)[a]
	1973	-25.5	-14.9
	1974	-12.7	-6.1
	1975	-9.4	-53.2
Gerald R. Ford[b]	1976	61.7	-88.4
	1977	-43.0	-53.7
Jimmy Carter	1978	-56.1	-59.2
	1979	-60.6	-40.7
	1980	-29.0	-73.8
	1981	-15.8	-79.0
Ronald Reagan	1982	-27.5	-128.0
	1983	-91.5	-207.8
	1984	-188.8	-185.4
	1985	-180.4	-212.3
	1986	-180.0	-221.2
	1987	-143.6	-149.8
	1988	-107.8	-155.2
	1989	-129.5	-152.6
George H. W. Bush	1990	-92.5	-221.0
	1991	-63.1	-269.2
	1992	-280.9	-290.3
	1993	-351.9	-255.0
William J. Clinton	1994	-254.7	-203.2
	1995	-176.1	-164.0
	1996	-196.7	-107.4
	1997	-168.8	-21.9
	1998	-120.6	69.3
	1999	9.5	125.6
	2000	117.3	236.2
	2001	184.0	128.2
George W. Bush	2002	231.2	-157.8
	2003	-80.2	-377.6
	2004	-307.4	-412.7
	2005	-363.6	-318.2
	2006	-390.1	-248.2
	2007	-354.2	-160.7

President	Fiscal Year	Projected Surplus (+)/Deficit(-)[a]	Actual Surplus(+)/ Deficit(-)[a]
	2008	-239.4	-458.6
	2009	-407.4	-1,412.7
Barack Obama	2010	-1,258.4	-1,555.6

Source: Figures for projected deficit are obtained from the budget message of the President in the Budget of the United States Government for each fiscal year as submitted in January of the previous calendar year. Figures for actual deficit are obtained from Budget of the United States Government FY2012. Historical Tables. Table 1.1—Summary of Receipts, Outlays, and Surpluses or Deficits: 1789-2016. Figures for FY1965-1968 are for the consolidated administrative and trust fund budgets. The figures for FY1969-1991 are for the unified budget. Figures for FY1992-2010 are for the total budget including Social Security, which was placed "off-budget" by the Budget Enforcement Act of 1990.

a. Surpluses are represented by a plus (+) sign.

b. Figures combine the amounts for FY1976 and the Transition Quarter that occurred when the start of the fiscal year was shifted from July 1 to October 1.

APPENDIX B. LEGISLATIVE HISTORY OF THE BALANCED BUDGET PROVISION IN 31 U.S.C. 1103

(formerly 31 U.S.C. 27)

"Byrd Amendment" (named after its sponsor Senator Harry F. Byrd, Jr. (D-VA))

Passed Senate 58-28 (vote no. 270, July 31, 1978), as an amendment to a bill to amend the Bretton Woods Agreement pertaining to the International Monetary Fund. The House adopted nonbinding instructions to its conferees on the bill that included agreeing to this provision, by a vote of 286-91 (roll no. 778, September 14, 1978). It was subsequently incorporated in the final version of the measure during conference.

The provision has been amended twice although there has been no separate vote in either chamber on these changes.

P.L. 95-435, 92 *Stat.* 1051, October 10, 1978

To amend the Bretton Woods Agreement (IMF).

(92 Stat. 1053) *"Section 7. Beginning with fiscal year 1981, the total budget outlays of the Federal Government shall not exceed its receipts."*

P.L. 96-389, 94 *Stat.* 1551, October 7, 1980

To amend the Bretton Woods Agreement (IMF).

(94 Stat. 1553) *"Section 3. Strike section 7 of P.L. 95-435, the Bretton Woods Agreements Act Amendments of 1978, which reads: 'Beginning with Fiscal Year 1981, the total budget outlays of the Federal Government shall not exceed its receipts.', and insert in lieu thereof: 'The Congress reaffirms its commitment that beginning with Fiscal Year 1981, the total budget outlays of the Federal Government shall not exceed its receipts.'"*

P.L. 97-258, 96 *Stat.* 877, September 13, 1982

To revise, codify and enact without substantive change certain general and permanent laws, related to money and finance, as title 31, United States Code, "Money and Finance."

(96 Stat. 908) *"Section 1103. Budget ceiling.*

Congress reaffirms its commitment that budget outlays of the United States Government for a fiscal year may not be more than the receipts of the Government for that year."

End Notes

[1] Letter from Thomas Jefferson to John Taylor, November 26, 1798. *The Writings of Thomas Jefferson*, vol. 10. (Washington: The Thomas Jefferson Memorial Association, 1903), p. 63.

[2] Herbert Stein, *The Fiscal Revolution in America*, rev. ed. (Washington: American Enterprise Press, 1990), p. 148.

[3] Ibid., p. 60.

[4] P.L. 304, 79th Congress, 60 *Stat.* 23.

[5] U.S. President, 1953-1961 (Eisenhower). The President's News Conference of February 18, 1959. *Public Papers of the Presidents of the United States, Dwight D. Eisenhower 1959* (Washington: GPO, 1960), p. 196.

[6] Ibid., p. 197.

[7] As early as 1966 economist Milton Friedman noted that "We are all Keynesians now and nobody is any longer a Keynesian." Quoted in Stein, *Fiscal Revolution*, p. 382, from *Time* (December 31, 1965, p. 65; and February 4, 1966, p. 13.).

[8] The report (S.Rept. 80-154) appears in the *Congressional Record*, vol. 93, May 6, 1947, at p. 4555.

[9] Although most states require their operating budget to be balanced they typically allow for debt financing of capital expenditures and various other exceptions to balanced budget requirements. For a examination of state balanced budget practices see U.S. General Accounting Office, *Balanced Budget Requirements: State Experiences and Implication for the Federal Government*, AFMD-93-58BR, March 1993.

[10] However, on several occasions Presidents have submitted proposed budgets that have included projections of balanced budgets at some point further in the future. President Carter's budget for FY1980 included projected balance for FY1982, his budget for FY1981 projected balance for FY1982 and FY1983, and his budget for FY1982 projected balance for FY1984. The amended FY1982 budget proposed by President Reagan also projected a balanced budget for FY1984 and extended the projection to include balanced budgets in FY1985 and FY1986. President Clinton's budget for FY1998 included a projected balanced budget for FY2002.

[11] For more information, see CRS Report R41778, *Reducing the Budget Deficit: Policy Issues*, by Marc Labonte.

[12] Quoted in U.S. Congress, Senate Committee on the Judiciary, *Balanced Budget Constitutional Amendment. Report on S.J.Res. 225,* S.Rept. 99-163, 99th Cong., 1st sess. (Washington: GPO, 1985), p. 3.

[13] U.S. President, 1981-1989 (Reagan), Inaugural Address, January 20, 1981, *Public Papers of the Presidents of the United States, Ronald Reagan 1981* (Washington: GPO, 1982), p. 2.

[14] U.S. President, 1981-1989 (Reagan), "Remarks Announcing America's Economic Bill of Rights," July 3, 1987. *Public Papers of the Presidents of the United States, Ronald Reagan 1987,* vol. I (Washington: GPO, 1987), p. 739.

[15] *Budget of the United States Government, FY1991* (Washington: GPO, 1990), p. 268.

[16] U.S. President, 1993- (Clinton), Letter to Congressional Leaders on the Proposed Balanced Budget Amendment, November 5, 1993, *Public Papers of the Presidents of the United States, William J. Clinton*, 1993, vol. II (Washington: GPO, 1994), p. 1916.

[17] H.Doc. 103-223, March 17, 1994.

[18] *Congressional Record*, daily edition, vol. 141(January 24, 1995), p. H586.

[19] "Text of President Clinton's State of the Union Message to Congress," *New York Times*, February 5, 1997, p. A20.

[20] Taylor, Andrew, "Governors: Don't Balance Budget Without Ending Mandates," *CQ Weekly Report*, November 26, 1994, p. 3403.

[21] "Budget Proposal Called 'Political Show,'" *Washington Post*, December 9, 1994, p. A18.

[22] Senator Mitch McConnell stated, "Our view is a good first step is a balanced budget amendment to the Constitution. All 47 Republicans are in favor of that," quoted in "GOP Conference on Balanced Budget," *CQ TranscriptsWire*, June 29, 2011, http://transcripts wire.cq.com/do/transcriptView?id=15591524.

[23] The White House, "Press Briefing by Press Secretary Jay Carney," press release, April 26, 2011, http://www.whitehouse.gov/the-press-office/2011/04/26/press-briefing-press-secretary- jay-carney-4262011.

[24] Judd Gregg, "Don't use amendment to dodge debt-ceiling action," *The Hill*, June 13, 2011.

[25] Tom Daschle, "The Trouble With the Balanced Budget Amendment," *The Wall Street Journal*, June 4, 2011.

[26] For example, in its 1982 study on balancing the federal budget, CBO reported that for half a century polling organizations have found that a large majority of Americans consistently had supported the idea of a balanced federal budget. See U.S. Congressional Budget Office, *Balancing the Federal Budget and Limiting Federal Spending: Constitutional and Statutory Approaches* (Washington: GPO, 1982), p. 28. (Hereinafter cited as CBO, *Balancing the Federal Budget.*) Other studies show similar results. See Andre Modigliani and F. Modigliani. "The Growth of the Federal Deficit and the Role of Public Attitudes," *Public Opinion Quarterly*, vol. 51, fall 1987.

[27] For a discussion of this phenomenon, see Andre Modigliani and F. Modigliani, "The Growth of the Federal Deficit and the Role of Public Attitudes."

[28] Senate Judiciary Committee, *Report on S.J.Res. 225*, p. 57.

[29] U.S. Congress. Senate Committee on the Judiciary. *Balanced Budget Constitutional Amendment. Report to Accompany S.J.Res. 41,* S.Rept. 103-163, 103rd Cong., 1st sess. (Washington: GPO, 1993), p. 6.

[30] For example, the Supreme Court has ruled that any alleged personal stake or injury must be direct and specific, not general. "A plaintiff must allege some particularized injury that sets him apart from the man on the street." *United States* v. *Richardson* 369 U.S. 186, 204 (1962). See also, *Valley Forge Christian College* v. *Americans United*, 454 U.S. 464, 483 (1982); *Allen* v. *Wright*, 468 U.S. 737, 754 (1984); *Whitmore* v. *Arkansas*, 495 U.S. 149 (1990); *Lujan* v. *Defenders of Wildlife*, 504 U.S. 555, 573-77 (1992); *Lance* v. *Coffman*, 549 U.S. 437, 441 (2007) (per curiam). *Cf. Ex parte Levitt*, 302 U.S. 633 (1937); *Laird* v. *Tatum*, 408 U.S. 1 (1972).

[31] *Frothingham* v. *Mellon*, 262 U.S. 447 (1923).

[32] 369 U.S. 186 (1962). As described in *United States* v. *Munoz-Flores*, 495 U.S. 385 (1990), "the political question doctrine is designed to restrain the judiciary from inappropriate interference in the business of the other branches of government." For a discussion of this doctrine, see Senate Judiciary Committee, *Report on S.J.Res. 225*, 99th Cong., 1st sess., p. 56.

[33] Alexander Hamilton, James Madison, and John Jay, *The Federalist Papers* (New York: Mentor Books, 1961), p. 465.

[34] Cited in Senate Judiciary Committee, *Report on S.J.Res. 225*, 99th Congress, 1st sess., p. 98.

[35] See remarks of Senator Mitchell in the *Congressional Record*, vol. 128, August 4, 1982, p. 19217.

[36] For a broader discussion of questions of justiciability, see Gay Aynesworth Crosthwait, "Article III Problems in Enforcing the Balanced Budget Amendment." *Columbia Law Review*, vol. 83, no. 5. June, 1983. p. 1065.

[37] *Allen* v. *Wright*, 468 U.S. 737 (1984).

[38] 495 U.S. 385 (1990).

[39] For a detailed discussion of State experience with balanced budget requirements, see Henning Bohn and Robert P. Inman, "Balanced Budget Rules and Public Deficits: Evidence From the U.S. States," *National Bureau of Economic Research Working Papers* no. 5533 (Cambridge, MA: National Bureau of Economic Research, 1996); Richard Briffault. *Balancing Acts: The Reality Behind State Balanced Budget Requirements* (Washington: Twentieth Century Fund Press, 1997); and Stewart E. Sterk and Elizabeth Goldman, "Controlling Legislative Shortsightedness: The Effectiveness of Constitutional Debt Limitations," *Wisconsin Law Review*, vol. 1991, no. 6. p. 1301.

[40] Senate Judiciary Committee, *Report on S.J.Res. 225*, 99th Cong., 1st sess. p. 96.

[41] CBO, *Balancing the Federal Budget*, p. 23, 103.

[42] P.L. 104-4, 109 *Stat.* 50, incorporated into the Congressional Budget Act at sections 421-428.

[43] The only previous proposed balanced budget amendment to be reported from a Committee was in 1947. A proposal introduced by Senators Millard Tydings (D-MD) and Styles Bridges (R-NH) was referred to the Senate Appropriations Committee by special arrangement. The Committee reported the proposal back to the Senate, but it was subsequently referred to the Senate Judiciary Committee and no further action was taken. (S.J.Res. 61, S.Rept. 154, 80th Congress; see *Congressional Record*, vol. 93, May 6, 1947. p. 4555-4557.)

[44] Detailed compilations of congressional committee hearings and floor actions for the 100th-103d Congresses have been prepared by the Senate Budget Committee. U.S. Congress. Senate. Committee on the Budget. *Proposed Constitutional Amendments to Balance the Federal Budget: Floor Action and Committee Hearings for the 100th Congress*. Committee Print S.Prt. 103-95, 103rd Cong., 2nd Sess. (Washington: GPO, 1994); U.S. Congress. Senate. Committee on the Budget. *Proposed Constitutional Amendments to Balance the Federal Budget: Floor Action and Committee Hearings for the 101st Congress*. Committee Print S.Prt. 103-94, 103rd Cong., 2nd Sess. (Washington: GPO, 1994); U.S. Congress. Senate. Committee on the Budget. *Proposed Constitutional Amendments to Balance the Federal Budget: Floor Action and Committee Hearings for the 102d Congress*. Committee Print S.Prt. 103-92, 103rd Cong., 2nd Sess. (Washington:GPO, 1994); U.S. Congress. Senate. Committee on the Budget. *Proposed Constitutional Amendments to Balance the Federal Budget: Floor Action and Committee Hearings for the 103d Congress*. Committee Print S.Prt. 103-112, 103rd Cong., 2nd Sess. (Washington: GPO, 1994).

[45] Senate consideration occurred on July 12, 13, 19, 26, 27, 28, 29, and 30 and August 2, 3, and 4, 1982. For the final vote see vote no. 288 in the *Congressional Record*, vol. 128, August 4, 1982, p. 19229.

[46] A king-of-the-hill rule is a variety of special rule which provides for the consideration of a series of alternatives regardless of the vote on any preceding alternative. Each alternative is

considered in a specified order and the last alternative agreed to is the one that is deemed finally agreed to.

[47] See vote no. 386 in the *Congressional Record*, daily edition, vol. 128 (October 1, 1982), p. H8336.

[48] See vote no. 387, ibid., p. H8337.

[49] Senate consideration occurred on March 6, 7, 10, 11, 12, 13, 18, and 25, 1986. For the final vote see vote no. 45 in the *Congressional Record*, daily edition, vol. 132 (March 25, 1986), p. S3345.

[50] See vote no. 236 in the *Congressional Record*, daily edition, vol. 136 (July 17, 1990), p. H4859.

[51] See vote no. 237, ibid., p. H4869.

[52] See vote no. 238, ibid., p. H4870.

[53] See vote no. 183 in the *Congressional Record*, daily edition, vol. 138 (June 11, 1992), p. H4605.

[54] See vote no. 184, ibid., p. H4621.

[55] See vote no. 185, ibid., p. H4637.

[56] See vote no. 186, ibid., p. H4660.

[57] See vote no. 187, ibid., p. H4670.

[58] See vote no. 133 in the *Congressional Record* (daily edition), vol. 138, June 30, 1992, p. S9219.

[59] See vote no. 134, ibid., p. S9243.

[60] See vote no. 47, in the *Congressional Record*, daily edition, vol. 140 (March 1, 1994), p. S2089.

[61] See vote no. 48, ibid., p. S2158.

[62] See vote no. 60 in the *Congressional Record*, daily edition, vol. 140 (March 16, 1994), p. H1413.

[63] See vote no. 64 in the *Congressional Record*, daily edition, vol. 140 (March 17, 1994), p. H1473.

[64] See vote no. 62, ibid., p. H1461.

[65] See vote no. 63, ibid, p. H1462. In the 103rd Congress the House adopted a rule (House Rule XII) which allowed the four territorial Delegates and the Resident Commissioner from Puerto Rico to vote in Committee of the Whole. However, a clause was also added to House Rule XXIII which provided that in a circumstance where their votes affected the outcome the Committee of the Whole would then rise and a new vote be taken in the House where neither the Delegates nor Resident Commissioner could vote.

[66] See vote no. 65 in the *Congressional Record*, daily edition, vol. 140 (March 17, 1994), p. H1497.

[67] See remarks of Representative Michael Flanagan in the *Congressional* Record, daily edition, vol. 141 (January 25, 1995), p. H619; H.Con.Res. 17 approved by vote no. 40, ibid., p. H628.

[68] This type of special rule was subsequently dubbed "queen-of-the-hill" by the press.

[69] See vote no. 41 in the *Congressional Record*, daily edition, vol. 141 (January 26, 1995), p. H713.

[70] See vote no. 43, ibid., p. H722.

[71] See vote no. 44, ibid., p. H731.

[72] See vote no. 46, ibid., p. H740.

[73] See vote no. 48, ibid., p. H753.

[74] See vote no. 49, ibid., p. H770.

[75] See vote no. 51, ibid., p. H772.

[76] "Amendment Vote Could Signal New Alliance." *Washington Post*. Jan. 28, 1995. p. A4.

[77] See the debate on the Harkin amendment (90) in the *Congressional Record*, daily edition, vol. 141 (January 26, 1995), p. S1557, 1583-1599.

[78] See vote no. 62 in the *Congressional Record*, daily edition, vol. 141 (February 8, 1995), p. S2307.

[79] See vote no. 65 in the *Congressional Record*, daily edition, vol. 141 (February 14, 1995), p. S2592.

[80] See vote no. 63 in the *Congressional Record*, daily edition, vol. 141 (February 10, 1995), p. S2453.

[81] See vote no. 74 in the *Congressional Record*, daily edition, vol. 141 (February 16, 1995), p. S2778.

[82] The remaining amendments and motions to be in order were enumerated, ibid., p. S2820.

[83] See vote no. 87 in the *Congressional Record*, daily edition, vol. 141 (February 28, 1995), p. S3276.

[84] See vote no. 98 in the *Congressional Record*, daily edition, vol. 141 (March 2, 1995), p. S3314.

[85] See vote no. 158 in the *Congressional Record*, daily edition, vol. 142 (June 6, 1996), p. S5903.

[86] Senate consideration occurred on February 5, 6, 7, 10, 11, 12, 13, 24, 25, 26, 27, and March 4. For the final vote, see vote no. 24 in the *Congressional Record*, daily edition, vol. 143 (March 4, 1997), p. S1920.

[87] For a general discussion, see CRS Report 95-589, *Amending the U.S. Constitution: by Congress or by Constitutional Convention*, by Thomas M. Durbin (out of print; available from the author upon request).

[88] Laurence H. Tribe, "Issues Raised by Requesting Congress to Call a Constitutional Convention to Propose a Balanced Budget Amendment." *Pacific Law Journal*, vol. 10, July 1979, p. 627.

[89] See, for example, Charles L. Black. "Amending the Constitution: A Letter to a Congressman," *Yale Law Journal*, v. 82, no. 2, December 1972. p. 189; William W. Van Alstyne, "Does Article V Restrict the States to Calling Unlimited Conventions Only?—A Letter to a Colleague," *Duke Law Journal*, vol. 1978, no. 6., December 1978. p. 1295; Walter E. Dellinger, "The Recurring Question of the 'Limited' Constitutional Convention," *Yale Law Journal*, vol. 88, no. 8, December 1979. p. 1623; and Michael Stokes Paulsen, "A General Theory of Article V: The Constitutional Lessons of the Twenty-seventh Amendment," *Yale Law Journal*, vol. 103, no. 8, December 1993. p. 677.

[90] For a broader discussion, see Durbin, *Amending the U.S. Constitution: by Congress or by Constitutional Convention*.

[91] U.S. Congress, House Committee on the Judiciary, Subcommittee on Civil and Constitutional Rights, *Constitutional Convention Procedures,* hearings, 99th Cong. 1st sess., July 31, September 23, 1985, serial no. 116.

[92] Ibid., p. 9.

[93] Information on state actions documented by Friends of the Article V Convention on their website at http://foavc.org/ file.php/1/Amendments.

[94] P.L. 95-435, 92 *Stat.* 1053.

[95] See vote no. 270 in the *Congressional Record*, vol. 124, July 31, 1978, p. 23411.

[96] The "Byrd amendment" originally appeared at 92 *Stat.* 1053 and was restated in 1980 in P.L. 96-389, 94 *Stat.* 1553. The most recent revision occurred in 1982 in P.L. 97-258, 96 *Stat.* 908. The text of these provisions appear in Appendix B.

[97] See vote no. 433 in the *Congressional Record*, daily edition, vol. 130 (October 2, 1984), p. H10858.

[98] See remarks of Representative Conable, ibid., p. H10662.

[99] See remarks of Representative Robert Walker (R-PA) in the *Congressional Record*, daily edition, vol. 136 (July 18, 1990), p. H4953.

[100] See remarks of Representative Panetta in the *Congressional Record*, daily edition, vol. 136 (July 18, 1990), p. H4950.

[101] See vote no. 246 in the *Congressional Record* (daily edition), v. 136, July 18, 1990, p. H4961.

[102] P.L. 99-177, 99 *Stat.* 1038-1101, also known as the Gramm-Rudman-Hollings Law. The Balanced Budget and Emergency Deficit Reduction Reaffirmation Act was contained in P.L. 100-119, 101 *Stat.* 754-784. For a description of these measures, see CRS Report R41901, *Statutory Budget Controls in Effect Between 1985 and 2002*, by Megan Suzanne Lynch.

[103] 106 S.Ct. 3181 (1986). A detailed analysis is in CRS Report 86-788, *Summary and Analysis of the Ramifications of Bowsher v. Synar, the Gramm-Rudman-Hollings Deficit Reduction Act Case*, by Morton Rosenberg and Richard Ehlke (out of print; available from the author upon request).

[104] For a discussion of the Budget Enforcement Act, see Lynch, *Statutory Budget Controls in Effect Between 1985 and 2002.*

[105] California, Connecticut, Delaware, Illinois, Iowa, Nebraska, New Hampshire, Pennsylvania, and Texas all have balanced budget requirements, but do not require end-of-year balance. In addition, Arizona, Georgia, Louisiana, Maryland, Massachusetts, New York, Utah, Virginia, Washington, and Wisconsin allow carryover and/or borrowing to finance a deficit if necessary. *Balanced Budget Requirements: State Experiences and Implications for the Federal Government*, GAO Report AFMD-93-58BR, p. 17.

[106] For example, such budget authority could be in the form of contract or entitlement authority for indefinite amounts of funds ("such sums as are necessary ...").

[107] Under current law (established in Section 13112(a)(4) of the Budget Enforcement Act) the President is required to submit the budget "On or after the first Monday in January but not later than the first Monday in February of each year."

[108] *Balanced Budget Requirements: State Experiences and Implications for the Federal Government*, GAO Report AFMD-93-58BR, p. 19.

[109] Senate Judiciary Committee, *Report to Accompany S.J.Res. 41*, 103rd Cong., 1st sess., p. 12.

[110] For more on federal debt see CRS Report R41815, *Overview of the Federal Debt*, by D. Andrew Austin and CRS Report RL34712, *The Federal Debt: An Analysis of Movements from World War II to the Present*, by Mindy R. Levit.

[111] U.S. Congressional Budget Office. *The Economic and Budget Outlook: Fiscal Years 2011-2021* (Washington: GPO, 2011), Table C-2, p. 125.

[112] The term *full faith and credit* is used to denote an explicit pledge to use the government's taxing authority to liquidate the debt.

[113] Sterk and Goldman, "Controlling Legislative Shortsightedness: The Effectiveness of Constitutional Debt Limitations."

[114] The Supreme Court, in *United States* v. *Munoz-Flores*, 495 U.S. 385 (1990), held that a requirement on federal Courts to impose a monetary "special assessment" on any person convicted of a federal misdemeanor was not a "bill for raising revenue."

Justice Story, in *Commentaries on the Constitution* (Boston, 1833. §880) wrote that only bills to raise taxes in the strict sense of the word are "bills for raising revenue;" bills for other purposes, which may incidentally create revenue, are not included. The Supreme Court later held, in *Twin City Bank* v. *Nebeker*, 167 U.S. 196 (1897) and *Millard* v. *Roberts*, 202 U.S. 429 (1906), that a bill that creates, and raises revenues to support, a particular governmental program, as opposed to a bill that raises revenue to support government generally, is not a "bill for raising revenue."

[115] Most periods of sustained surpluses were a result of a deliberate policy to buy down the debt. Examples of this occurred after federal assumption of state debts associated with the Revolution, and repayment of debts associated with the Civil War. Sustained surpluses in the absence of such specific aims were politically difficult. For example, surpluses generated by tariff policy of the late 19th century provoked debates about whether tariff rates should be lowered or expenditures increased in order to eliminate the surplus. For more on this period, see John F. Cogan. "The Evolution of Congressional Budget Decisionmaking and the Emergence of Federal Deficits." *Working Papers in Political Science* no. P-88-6 (Palo Alto: The Hoover Institution, 1988); and Charles Haines Stewart. *Budget Reform*

Politics: The Design of the Appropriations Process in the House of Representatives, 1865-1921 (Cambridge [U.K.]: Cambridge University Press, 1989).

[116] For more on tax expenditures generally, see CRS Report RL34622, *Tax Expenditures and the Federal Budget*, by Thomas L. Hungerford.

[117] Federal courts do not issue opinions that are merely advisory. Declaratory judgments, according to *Aetna Life Ins. Co.* v. *Haworth*, 300 U.S. 227, 241 (1937), are issued in cases of "real and substantial controversy admitting of specific relief through a decree of a conclusive character, as distinguished from an opinion advising what the law would be upon a hypothetical state of facts."

[118] In *Marbury* v. *Madison*, 1 Cr. (5 U.S.) 137 (1803) Chief Justice John Marshall asserted the Supreme Court's power of judicial review, stating that it was "too extravagant to be maintained that the Framers had intended that a case arising under the constitution should be decided without examining the instrument under which it arises." For more on judicial review see Louis Fisher and Katy J. Harrieger. *American Constitutional Law* (9th ed.) (Durham: Carolina Academic Press, 2011), chapter 2.

In: Federal Budget Control
Editors: D. Groff and B. Rutherford
ISBN: 978-1- 61942-051-9

Chapter 2

TESTIMONY OF CONGRESSMAN BOB GOODLATTE SUBCOMMITTEE ON THE CONSTITUTION MAY 13, 2011

Bob Goodlatte

March 2, 1995 was a pivotal day in the history of our country. On that day, the U.S. Senate failed by one vote to send a balanced budget amendment to the states for ratification. The amendment had passed the House by the required 2/3rd majority previously and the Senate vote was the last legislative hurdle before ratification by the states.

If that amendment had passed, then we would not be facing the fiscal crisis we now face. If that amendment had passed, then balancing the budget would have been the norm, rather than the exception over the past 25 years and we would have nothing like the annual deficits and skyrocketing debt that we must address today.

The good news is that like 1995, this Congress is again standing at a crossroads at this very moment. The decisions we make today will steer the direction of the country for the next 25 years. We have an opportunity now to take action to ensure that 25 years from today, our children will face a much brighter fiscal picture. We must not allow ourselves to miss this opportunity.

Here's what we know: experience has proven time and again that Congress cannot for any significant length of time rein in excessive spending. The annual deficits and the resulting debt continue to grow due to political pressures and dependency on government programs.

Budget plans that purport to cut spending over long periods of time are great goals, but in order to achieve the results these budgets promise, a majority of fiscally conservative Members must be elected into perpetuity. While it is one of my strongest desires that this will occur, we simply cannot afford to bet our children and grandchildren's future on this happening.

In order for Congress to be able to consistently make the very tough decisions necessary to sustain fiscal responsibility over the long term, Congress must have an external pressure to force it to do so.

I believe that the most realistic chance we have today to enact the institutional reform necessary is through a balanced budget amendment to our Constitution.

Many Members of Congress have introduced balanced budget amendments this Congress. I introduced two versions on the first day of the 112th Congress. H.J.Res. 2 is the exact text that passed the House in 1995 and failed in the Senate by one vote. This amendment requires that total annual outlays not exceed total annual receipts. It also requires a true majority of each chamber to pass tax increases and requires a 3/5 majority to raise the debt limit. This legislation also has limited exceptions for times of war.

H.J.Res. 1, which I also introduced, goes much further. In addition to the provisions of H.J.Res. 2, it also requires a 3/5 majority to raise taxes and imposes an annual spending cap that prohibits spending from exceeding 20% of GDP.

In the U.S. Senate, 47 Republican Senators have cosponsored a balanced budget amendment that is similar to H.J.Res. 1, which is a strong sign that the Senate is ready to engage in debate on this subject.

While my preference is to pass the stronger version of the balanced budget amendment, I want to be very clear in my testimony today. The 2/3 majority requirement for passing an amendment to the Constitution demands that we achieve bipartisan support for any balanced budget amendment.

Our extraordinary fiscal crisis demands an extraordinary solution, so we simply cannot afford to succumb to political posturing on this issue at a point in time so critical to our nation's future. We must rise above that and move forward with a strategy that includes legislation that will get at least 290 votes on the House Floor.

So, as we consider a balanced budget amendment, I encourage the Members of this Committee to devote our effort to passing the strongest balanced budget amendment that can garner 2/3 of the House of Representatives.

We are at a crossroads in America. We can make the tough choices and control spending, paving the way for a return to surpluses and ultimately paying down the national debt, or we can allow big spenders to lead us further down the road of chronic deficits and leave our children and grandchildren saddled with debt that is not their own.

The choice is ours. The stakes are high. Failure is not an option.

In: Federal Budget Control
Editors: D. Groff and B. Rutherford
ISBN: 978-1- 61942-051-9

Chapter 3

SHOULD THE CONSTITUTION BE AMENDED TO ADDRESS THE FEDERAL DEFICIT? MAY 13, 2011

David M. Primo

Good Morning Chairman Franks, Ranking Member Nadler, and members of the subcommittee. Thank you for inviting me here this morning to discuss whether the U.S. Constitution should be amended to address the nation's fiscal problems.

I am an associate professor of political science at the University of Rochester and a senior scholar at the Mercatus Center at George Mason University.[1] My research focuses on legislative politics and fiscal policy. I have written papers and a book on the subject of budget rules, and I have been following the debate over our nation's future fiscal course with great interest.[2] In my testimony, I will show why attempts to create long-term fiscal reform, stabilize the debt, and reduce the deficit are likely to fail in the absence of Constitutional budget rules.

The United States faces severe fiscal challenges that can no longer be ignored. Our current $14 trillion national debt is just the tip of the iceberg. Entitlement spending threatens to bankrupt the nation. The unfunded liabilities from Social Security and Medicare are three to seven times the size of our current debt, depending on how one calculates these figures.[3]

Any solution to this crisis must accomplish three things: First, Social Security and Medicare expenses have to be stabilized and future promises have to be limited. Second, discretionary spending has to be pared down. Third, future politicians must be prevented from undoing any reforms that are implemented. The focus of my testimony today will be the third of these requirements.

The recent bipartisan attention to the challenges we face is heartening. The dangers of our debt and deficit levels are no longer the province of commissions whose reports gather dust. Instead, we have elected officials taking a stand and proposing bold changes to the status quo. The President's National Commission on Fiscal Responsibility and Reform proposed a serious plan, and legislators from both parties endorsed it. House Budget Committee Chairman Paul Ryan proposed an ambitious plan to control federal spending, and President Barack Obama responded to Chairman Ryan's plan with one of his own. Voters are also paying attention. In a poll conducted by Pew Research Center and *TheWashington Post* in April 2011, an astonishing 95% of respondents agreed that the federal budget deficit was a problem, and 81% agreed that action was needed now.[4]

This, in short, is a rare opportunity for meaningful long-term change. I believe that a Constitutional amendment can help us avoid making this a wasted opportunity. In my testimony, I will first establish that opportunities for long-term fiscal reforms rarely emerge. I will then show why long-term reforms are unlikely to be robust without Constitutional change. The next part of my testimony will focus on why it is important to get the rules right and offer some principles that I hope members will follow as they work toward achieving fiscal discipline. I will close my testimony by rebutting arguments against a Constitutional amendment.

THE CHALLENGES OF FISCAL REFORM

The enactment of real fiscal reform is always an uphill battle. Three factors stack the deck against reform:

- Fiscal problems are "creeping" risks.
- The electoral benefits of additional spending typically exceed the electoral benefits of fiscal discipline.
- Pledges made by legislators today will be hard to keep tomorrow.

Creeping Risks

Creeping risks, also referred to as slow failures, develop gradually over time, with any single event having a small but real effect on risk severity.[5] As enough events occur, the risk ultimately manifests itself in catastrophic ways. The World Economic Forum identifies fiscal crises as one of the major creeping risks facing the world today, and the recent debt crisis in Greece is an excellent example of a creeping risk manifesting itself suddenly.[6] The U.S. fiscal situation, though perhaps not as dire as Greece's right now, is headed in the same direction.

The temptation when dealing with creeping risks, as opposed to immediate risks, is to postpone action. A bullet to the chest is an immediate risk for which delayed action is not an option. A poor diet, which could eventually lead to heart disease, is a creeping risk. It's easy to avoid action on a diet. It's not so easy to avoid dealing with a bullet wound. The same is true of the federal budget. Many of the most severe risks we face, including the trajectory of Medicare spending, will not manifest themselves in dramatic fashion for years, prompting many legislators and pundits to argue that tough decisions should be postponed, as well. Unfortunately, the longer we wait to address creeping risks, the bigger the costs will be.

Fortunately, recent statements from legislators in both parties, as well as the president, acknowledge that we ought to take on long-term fiscal problems. To be sure, there are passionate disagreements about how to address these problems. But even agreement that a problem exists is progress.

Electoral Benefits of Spending

The nature of government spending makes it important to take advantage of the current realization that budget reform is needed. The benefits of government programs are typically much more concentrated than the costs of those programs.[7] If spending and taxes are reduced by $1 billion through cuts to construction projects, each citizen receives about $3 in benefits through lower taxes, but the beneficiaries of the construction projects lose far more per capita. It is much easier for a member of Congress to claim credit for preserving the construction project than to claim credit for the savings from eliminating such a project. The politics of fiscal reform, then, are stacked in favor of beneficiaries over taxpayers. Typically, beneficiaries will be the winners, and taxpayers the losers. Curiously, though, economists have found that elected officials who spearhead fiscal adjustments (a sustained decrease in deficit-to-GDP or debt-to-GDP ratio) are not typically punished at the ballot box.[8] This is a puzzle until one realizes that fiscal adjustments are "endogenous," or chosen strategically by politicians. Researchers have also shown that fiscal adjustments are often spurred on by crises, when the public may be willing to accept tough medicine.[9] So, in the face of an active crisis (or the perception that a crisis is imminent), the political calculi that prevent reform may be adjusted in favor of taxpayers. As I noted earlier, elected officials may have more leeway today than in most years. The public is paying attention to the deficit and believes some action is needed, though just as in Congress, there is disagreement among voters regarding how to achieve fiscal reform.

Keeping Promises

Acknowledgment by Congress and President Obama that creeping fiscal risks have to be addressed, and public agreement in this regard, creates a rare opportunity for change. Without an enforcement mechanism to accompany any reform agreements, there is a significant risk that any promises made today will not be kept tomorrow. Legislators may commit today to cutting spending next year (and the following year, and so on), but when next year comes, legislators and their constituents may value spending over the cut, especially if the cut is painful. In other words, the same pain the legislator is trying to avoid today will manifest itself next year, forcing the same difficult choice. The political reality is that the hard cuts in any plan are usually deferred until well into the future, so the likelihood of long-term agreements having durability in the absence of some external enforcement mechanism is very small.

We can make an analogy to somebody trying to lose ten pounds. This person could write out a plan for doing so, but without some enforcement mechanism, the temptation each day would be to skip a workout or eat that extra piece of dessert. Just as somebody trying to lose weight needs some sort of enforcement mechanism to achieve his or her goal, any agreement on budget reform requires a similar enforcement mechanism.

THE CASE FOR CONSTITUTIONAL CHANGE

There are many ways to create enforcement mechanisms to ensure that agreements reached today are enforced tomorrow. The House and the Senate can create internal enforcement rules, such as the PAYGO rules passed in 2007. Congress and the president can reach agreement on a statute with enforcement mechanisms, as with Gramm-Rudman-Hollings legislation in the 1980s. Or, these rules can be codified in the Constitution. Constitutional rules are the only ones, however, that are "sticky" in the short-run and therefore immune to the problems that plague internal or statutory rules.

Article I, Section V of the U.S. Constitution establishes why chamber-based and even statutory rules are inferior to Constitutional rules. It states plainly, "Each House may determine the rules of its proceedings." The implications of this simple statement are profound. Members of Congress can construct their own rules, meaning that they can change their own rules, or even ignore them, as they see fit. The current Congress cannot bind future Congresses. If the goal of a rule is to ensure that deals are kept, some external enforcement mechanism is needed.

Statutes may provide slightly more durability than internal rules, but these can be changed with a simple majority vote if the president chooses not to veto a change. And when Congress is feeling enough pressure from constituents that they want to abrogate a budget agreement, it will be difficult for the president to stand in its way. Historically, we have observed Congress and the president evade or undo rules that proved to be inconvenient. Gramm-Rudman-Hollings and PAYGO are two examples.[10]

Constitutional rules are different. Unlike internal or statutory rules, Constitutional rules can only be changed after several significant hurdles are overcome, including either a two-thirds majority in the House and the Senate or a Constitutional convention, either of which would have to be followed by ratification of the change by three-fourths of the states. By contrast, internal or statutory rules can be changed in days, minutes even, if the political will exists. Constitutional rules typically take years to change, and changes are rare, as evidenced by the small number of amendments—27—to the U.S. Constitution. Moreover, the U.S. Supreme Court would be able to intervene if Congress flouted Constitutional budget rules.

Constitutional rules, therefore, provide the means to help keep Congress in check and ensure that fiscal discipline is maintained even when the temptation to abrogate agreements is hard to resist. Statutory rules and internal rules simply do not provide the same level of stability. If Congress is committed to long-term fiscal reform, it ought to propose to the states a Constitutional amendment that creates a framework for fiscal discipline.

Getting the Rules Right

The promise of Constitutional rules as enforcement mechanisms lies in their durability. But this durability is also a peril: bad rules can be locked-in just as good rules can be. I will discuss three principles of rule design that will help mitigate this problem.

1. Legislators should design budget rules that are general and apply to the entire federal budget.
   A Constitutional rule is meant to be permanent, and as a consequence, it should focus on total federal spending or revenues rather than specific government programs. A Constitutional amendment regarding the Medicare program, for instance, is ill-advised. An amendment that limits the outlays or the revenues of the federal government speaks to a general principle of fiscal responsibility, and it provides the structure for subsequent debates in Congress about how to achieve that principle. Moreover, it prevents legislators from carving out certain programs from this general principle, as is often done today with entitlements like Medicare and Social Security.
2. Legislators should design rules that are precise and prevent the use of loopholes or gimmicks.
   Budget rules ostensibly designed to accomplish the same goal, perhaps even with the same name, can have very different effects depending on how they are implemented. Yet, budget rules are often (intentionally) written in vague terms, with the details left to be worked out. Or, the wording of the rule permits evasion relatively easily. The details can make-or-breaka rule's effectiveness, since the entire purpose of rules is to encourage elected officials to take actions that they have incentives not to take. Definitions are crucial in this regard. For instance, Congress allowed itself to determine on a case-by-case basis what constituted an emergency that permitted caps on spending or PAYGO laws to be waived.[11]Constitutional rules that leave implementation details up to Congress may be eviscerated once the details are worked out.

3. Legislators should design rules with limited, carefully constructed exit options.

   While the point of a Constitutional rule is durability, unexpected events require that Congress has the flexibility to, say, fund a war or handle a major emergency. To address such emergencies, most Constitutional budget rule proposals permit waiver of the rule with either a majority, three-fifths, or two-thirds supermajority. These thresholds are problematic because they are no more difficult than passing regular legislation, circumventing a filibuster, or overriding a presidential veto, respectively.

   In order to send a signal that Constitutional rules ought to be waived only in extraordinary circumstances, the threshold for waiving the rules should be very high—say, 90% of both chambers. In true emergencies, the Congress would undoubtedly provide needed funds. In order to make the declaration of an emergency transparent, spending made under this provision could be segregated from other spending and be paid back during a set time period—for instance, 10 or 15 years. This would further discourage inappropriate use of waiver provisions.[12]

ARGUMENTS AGAINST CONSTITUTIONAL BUDGET RULES, AND MY REPLIES

Amending the Constitution is a serious—some might even say drastic—step for the country, and there is strong opposition to taking this action on budgetary matters. I will now consider three important arguments against reform and rebut them.

1. **Claim:** A Constitutional amendment is unnecessary since all we need to do to restore fiscal discipline is pass the right kinds of bills.

   Reply: In a perfect world, this claim would be absolutely correct. Legislators and the president would come together and agree to binding limits on spending, and then they would live by those agreements. Voters would understand when significant cuts to local projects were required or when Medicare benefits were scaled back. In the real world, however, such agreements are unlikely to survive for more than a few years before elected officials succumb to spending temptations.

2. **Claim:**A Constitutional amendment gives too much power to the U.S. Supreme Court over budgetary matters.
   Reply: Unless an amendment explicitly rules this out (as some versions of Constitutional budget rules do), the U.S. Supreme Court may adjudicate disputes regarding Constitutional budget rules, and lawsuits challenging Congressional budgets may be commonplace. The end result, some fear, is a budget process that ends each year with the decision of nine unelected justices. This fear is unwarranted, as rule designers can be proactive in limiting judicial overreach. The Supreme Court could be authorized to require only certain sorts of remedies—for instance, the Court could only mandate spending cuts to satisfy a balanced budget rule, not tax increases. Standing of citizens could be limited to avoid frivolous lawsuits. And, the clearer the rule, the less leeway the justices will have in interpreting it. This fear of judicial intervention, in fact, will motivate Congress to take all possible actions to avoid Court involvement in the budget process. Moreover, the Court will be loath to micromanage the budget process, and would most likely simply request that a problematic budget be revised. The hypothetical dangers outlined by critics of Constitutional reform have to be balanced against the very real danger that Congress will not be able to abide by the rules it sets out for itself, or will change them when the going gets tough.
3. **Claim:**A Constitutional budget rule won't solve our fiscal problems, but will merely shift burdens to the states.
   Reply: A Constitutional budget rule will certainly force the states to reevaluate their spending habits, but this is a benefit, not a drawback, of such a rule. By placing spending decisions closer to the people who have to bear the costs of those decisions, policy outcomes will tend to be more efficient. Limits on federal spending, and especially aid to the states, will also eliminate incentives for states to overspend. There is extensive evidence in the economics literature for a "flypaper effect," meaning that federal aid tends to "stick where it hits" and create upward pressure on state spending.[13] Though there is dispute about the precise size of this flypaper effect, there is little doubt that federal aid creates perverse incentives for the states.

CLOSING

In closing, Congress and the president have a rare opportunity to enact meaningful budget reforms. My fear is that those agreements will ultimately dissolve in the absence of a Constitutional amendment that provides a framework for enforcing those agreements. Constitutional rules, unlike statutory or internal rules, are difficult to change. If written to cover the entire budget, avoid loopholes, and make waivers difficult to obtain, Constitutional rules can provide the enforcement mechanism that willhelp ensure that specific reforms to entitlements, defense, and other spending areas will not be undone by future Congresses.

Thank you again for inviting me to testify. I welcome your questions.

End Notes

[1] The views expressed here are my own and do not represent the official positions of the University of Rochester or the Mercatus Center at George Mason University.

[2] See, for example, Primo, David M. 2007. *Rules and Restraint: Government Spending and the Design of Institutions*. American Politics and Political Economy Series. Chicago, IL: University of Chicago Press. Some passages and ideas in this testimony appear in Primo, David M. 2010. "Making Budget Rules Work." Working Paper No. 10-62, Mercatus Center at George Mason University, available at http://mercatus.org/sites/default/files/publication/ Making%20Budget%20Rules%20Work.Primo .9.28.10.pdf.

[3] Board of Trustees of the Federal Old-Age and Survivors Insurance and Federal Disability Insurance Trust Funds. 2009. *Annual Report*. Washington, DC: Government Printing Office; Boards of Trustees of the Federal Hospital Insurance and Federal Supplementary Medical Insurance Trust Funds. 2009. *Annual Report*. Washington, DC: Government Printing Office. The Medicare Trustees set unfunded obligations for Part B and D at 0 because they are guaranteed funding from general revenues. However, the portion of Part B and D that comes out of general revenues can reasonably be construed as an unfunded liability, since specific revenues are not allocated for this spending (as opposed to Social Security, for which there is a dedicated fund); if these costs are accounted for, unfunded liabilities exceed $100 trillion dollars.

[4] See http://people-press.org/files/legacy-questionnaires/4-26-11%20Topline%20for%20release %20with%20joint%20WaPo%20deficit%20questions.pdf.

[5] Global Risk Network of the World Economic Forum. 2010. *Global Risks 2010: A Global Risk Network Report*. Geneva, Switzerland: World Economic Forum.

[6] Ibid.

[7] Wilson, James Q. 1980. *The Politics of Regulation*. New York: Basic Books; Lowi, Theodore J. 1964. "American Business, Public Policy, Case-Studies, and Political Theory." *World Politics* 16:677-693.

[8] Alesina, Alberto. 2010. "Fiscal Adjustments: What Do We Know and What Are We Doing?" Working Paper No. 10-61, Mercatus Center at George Mason University, available at http://mercatus.org/sites/default/files/publication/Fiscal%20Adjustments.%20What%20Do.. Corrected%20Table.Alesina .pdf; Alesina, Alberto, Roberto Perotti, and Jose Tavares.

1998. "The Political Economy of Fiscal Adjustments." *Brookings Papers on Economic Activity* 1998(1):197-266.

[9] Alesina, Alberto, Silvia Ardagna, and Francesco Trebbi. 2006. "Who Adjusts and When? The Political Economy of Reforms." *IMF Staff Papers* 53(Special Issue):1-29.

[10] For a description of the pitfalls of PAYGO, see de Rugy, Veronique, and David Bieler. 2010. "Is PAYGO a No-Go?" Mercatus on Policy No. 73, Mercatus Center at George Mason University, available at http://mercatus.org/sites/default/files/publication/MOP73 PAYGO web.pdf.

[11] Saturno, James V. 2007. "Emergency Spending: Statutory and Congressional Rules." CRS Report for Congress, RS21035, July 24.

[12] For several examples of questionable emergency designations, see de Rugy, Veronique. 2008. "The Never-Ending Emergency: Trends in Supplemental Spending." Mercatus Policy Series Policy Comment No. 18, Mercatus Center at George Mason University, available at http://mercatus.org/sites/default/files/publication/The Never-Ending Emergency.pdf.

[13] For an overview, see Hines, Jr., James R., and Richard H. Thaler. 1995. "Anomalies: The Flypaper Effect." *Journal of Economic Perspectives* 9(4):217–26; Inman, Robert P. 2008. "The Flypaper Effect." NBER Working Paper No. 14579.

In: Federal Budget Control
Editors: D. Groff and B. Rutherford

ISBN: 978-1- 61942-051-9

Chapter 4

Testimony of Robert Greenstein President, Center on Budget and Policy Priorities before the House Judiciary Committee May 13, 2011

Robert Greenstein

Thank you for the invitation to testify today. I am Robert Greenstein, president of the Center on Budget and Policy Priorities, a policy institute that focuses both on fiscal policy and on policies affecting low- and moderate-income Americans. We, like most others who analyze fiscal policy developments and trends, believe that the nation's fiscal policy is on an unsustainable course. As part of our work, we have been analyzing proposed changes in budget procedures for more than 20 years. We have conducted extensive analyses of proposals to write a balanced-budget requirement into the Constitution, among other proposals.

The purpose of changing our fiscal policy course is to strengthen our economy over the long term and to prevent the serious economic damage that would likely occur if the debt explodes in future decades as a share of the economy. But we need to choose our fiscal policy instruments carefully. We want to avoid "destroying the village in order to save it."

The goal of a constitutional balanced budget amendment is to address our long-term fiscal imbalance. Unfortunately, a constitutional balanced budget amendment would be a highly ill- advised way to try to do that and likely would cause serious economic damage. It would require a balanced budget every year regardless of the state of the economy, unless a supermajority of both houses overrode that requirement. This is an unwise stricture that many mainstream economists have long counseled against, because it would require the largest budget cuts or tax increases precisely when the economy is weakest. It holds substantial risk of tipping faltering economies into recessions and making recessions longer and deeper. The additional job losses would likely be very large.

When the economy weakens, revenue growth drops and revenues may even contract. And as unemployment rises, expenditures for programs like unemployment insurance — and to a lesser degree, food stamps and Medicaid — increase. These revenue declines and expenditure increases are temporary; they largely disappear as the economy recovers. But they are critical for helping struggling economies to keep from falling into a recession and for moderating the depth and length of recessions that do occur.

When the economy weakens, consumers and businesses spend less, which in turn causes further job loss. The drop in tax collections and increases in unemployment and other benefits that occur automatically when the economy weakens cushions the blow, by keeping purchases of goods and services from falling more. That is why economists use the term "automatic stabilizers" to describe the automatic declines in revenues and automatic increases in UI and other benefits that occur when the economy turns down; these actions help to stabilize the economy.

A constitutional balanced budget amendment, however, effectively suspends the automatic stabilizers. It requires that federal expenditures be cut or taxes increased to offset the effects of the automatic stabilizers and prevent a deficit from occurring — the opposite course from what sound economic policy calls for.

Over the years, leading economists have warned of the adverse effects of a constitutional balanced budget amendment. For example, in Congressional testimony in 1992, Robert Reischauer — then director of the Congressional Budget Office and one of the nation's most respected experts on fiscal policy — explained: "[I] f it worked [a constitutional balanced budget amendment] would undermine the stabilizing role of the federal government." Reischauer noted that the automatic stabilizing that occurs when the economy is weak "temporarily lowers revenues and increases spending on unemployment insurance and welfare programs. This automatic stabilizing occurs quickly and is self-limiting — it goes away as the economy revives — but it temporarily increases the deficit. It is an important factor that dampens the amplitude of our economic cycles." Under the constitutional amendment, he explained, these stabilizers would no longer operate automatically.[1]

Similarly, when a constitutional balanced budget amendment was under consideration in 1997, more than 1,000 economists including 11 Nobel laureates issued a joint statement that said, "We condemn the proposed 'balanced-budget' amendment to the federal Constitution. It is unsound and unnecessary. ... The proposed amendment mandates perverse actions in the face of recessions. In economic downturns, tax revenues fall and some outlays, such as unemployment benefits, rise. These so-called "built-in stabilizers' limit declines of after-tax income and purchasing power. To keep the budget balanced every year would aggravate recessions."[2]

More recently, in January 2011, the current CBO director, Douglas Elmendorf, sounded a similar warning when asked about a constitutional balanced budget amendment at a Senate Budget Committee hearing. Elmendorf observed:

> "Amending the Constitution to require this sort of balance raises risks .... [t]he fact that taxes fall when the economy weakens and spending and benefit programs increase when the economy weakens, in an automatic way, under existing law, is an important stabilizing force for the aggregate economy. The fact that state governments need to work ... against these effects in their own budgets — need to take action to raise taxes or cut spending in recessions — undoes the automatic stabilizers, essentially, at the state level. Taking those away at the federal level risks making the economy less stable, risks exacerbating the swings in business cycles."[3]

Proponents of a constitutional amendment likely will respond to these admonitions by noting that the proposed constitutional amendment would allow the balanced-budget requirement to be waived by a vote of three-fifths of the House and the Senate. That, however, does not address this problem. It is difficult to secure three-fifths votes for anything; consider the paralysis that marks the work of the Senate. Moreover, it may take months after a downturn begins before sufficient data are available to convince three-fifths of the members of both houses of Congress that a recession is underway. Furthermore, it is all too likely that even after the evidence for a downturn is clear, a minority in the House or Senate would hold a wavier vote hostage to demands for concessions on other matters (such as new, permanent tax cuts). By the time a recession were recognized to be underway and three-fifths votes were secured in both chambers, if such support could be obtained at all, extensive economic damage could have been done and hundreds of thousands or millions of additional jobs unnecessarily lost.

The bottom line is that the automatic stabilizers need to continue to be able to work automatically to protect American businesses and workers. The balanced budget amendment precludes that.

Nor is a recession the only concern. Consider the savings and loan crisis of the 1980s, or the financial meltdown of the fall of 2008. A constitutional balanced budget amendment would have hindered swift federal action to rescue the savings and loan industry or to rapidly put the Troubled Assets Relief Program in place. In both cases, history indicates that federal action helped save the economy from what otherwise likely would have been far more dire problems.

Moreover, the federal government provides deposit insurance for accounts of up to $250,000; this insurance — and the confidence it engenders among depositors — is critical to the sound functioning of our financial system so that we avoid panics involving a run on financial institutions, as occurred in the early 1 930s. A constitutional prohibition of any deficit spending (unless and until a supermajority of both houses of Congress voted to authorize it) could seriously weaken the guarantee that federal deposit insurance provides. That is a risk we should not take.

These are illustrations of why fiscal policy should not be written into the Constitution.

A parallel problem is that the proposed constitutional amendment would make it even harder than it already is to raise the debt limit, by requiring a three-fifths vote of both the House and Senate to raise the limit. This is playing with fire. It would heighten the risk of a federal government default. A default would raise our interest costs and could damage the U.S. economy for years to come.

Mistaken Analogies to States and Families

Proponents of a constitutional amendment sometimes argue that states and families must balance their budgets every year and the federal government should do so, too. But statements that the constitutional amendment would align federal budgeting practices with those of states and families are not accurate.

While states must balance their *operating* budgets, they can borrow to finance their *capital* budgets — to finance roads, schools, and other projects.

Most states do so. States also can build reserves during good times and draw on them in bad times *without* counting the drawdown from reserves as new spending that unbalances a budget.

Families follow similar practices. They borrow — they take out mortgages to buy a home or student loans to send a child to college. They also draw down savings when times are tight, with the result that their expenditures in those periods exceed their current incomes.

But the proposed constitutional amendment would bar such practices at the federal level. The *total* federal budget — including capital investments — would have to be balanced every year, with no borrowing allowed for infrastructure or other investments that can boost future economic growth. And if the federal government ran a surplus one year, it could *not* draw it down the next year to help balance the budget.

I would also note that the fact that states must balance their operating budgets even in recessions makes it all the more important from the standpoint of economic policy that the federal government *not* be subject to the same stricture. American Enterprise Institute analyst Norman Ornstein addressed this matter in a recent article, where he wrote: "Few ideas are more seductive on the surface and more destructive in reality than a balanced budget amendment. Here is why: Nearly all our states have balanced budget requirements. That means when the economy slows, states are forced to raise taxes or slash spending at just the wrong time, providing a fiscal drag when what is needed is countercyclical policy to stimulate the economy. In fact, the fiscal drag from the states in 2009-2010 was barely countered by the federal stimulus plan. That meant the federal stimulus provided was nowhere near what was needed but far better than doing nothing. Now imagine that scenario with a federal drag instead."[4]

H.J. Res. 1 Raises Additional Issues

The foregoing concerns apply to all versions of the balanced budget amendment that have been introduced. Some versions of the balanced budget amendment, such as H.J. Res 1, raise additional serious concerns, because they would write into the Constitution new prohibitions against raising any revenues — including closing wasteful tax loopholes — to help balance the budget and also would prohibit federal expenditures in any year from exceeding a figure such as 20 percent of the Gross Domestic Product. These constitutional prohibitions could be overridden only by supermajority votes in both the House and the Senate.

This requirement for a supermajority to raise taxes would be extremely unsound. It would protect what President Reagan's former chief economic advisor, Harvard economist Martin Feldstein, has called the biggest area of wasteful government spending in the federal budget — what economists call "tax expenditures" and Alan Greenspan has called "tax entitlements."

In 2010, tax expenditures amounted to $1.1 trillion, more than the cost of Medicare and Medicaid combined (which was $719 billion), Social Security ($701 billion), defense ($689 billion, including expenditures in Iraq and Afghanistan), or non-defense discretionary spending ($658 billion, including expenditures from the Recovery Act). Many of these tax expenditures are fully the equivalent of government spending. Let me use child care as an example.

If you are low- or moderate-income, you may get a federal subsidy to help cover your child care costs, and the subsidy is provided through a spending program. If you are higher on the income scale, you still get a government subsidy that reduces your child care costs, but it is delivered through the tax code, as a tax credit. (Moreover, if you are a low or modest income parent with child care costs, you likely will miss out because the spending programs that provide child care subsidies are *not* open ended and can only serve as many people as their capped funding allows. By contrast, if you are a higher income household — and there is no limit on how high your income can be — your child care subsidy is *guaranteed*, because the tax subsidy you get operates as an open-ended entitlement.) It is difficult to justify making the tax-code subsidy sacrosanct and the program subsidy a deficit-reduction target merely because one is delivered through a "spending" program and the other is delivered through the code.

And as the child care example illustrates, sharply distinguishing between subsidies delivered through the tax code and those delivered through programs on the spending side of the budget also has a "reverse Robin Hood" aspect. Low- and moderate-income households receive most of their government assistance through spending programs; affluent households receive most of their federal subsidies through tax expenditures. Effectively barring reductions in tax expenditures from contributing to deficit reduction is a prescription for placing the greatest burden of deficit reduction on those who can least afford to bear it.

The problems do not stop there. If it requires a supermajority to raise any revenue, another likely outcome is a proliferation of tax loopholes. New loopholes — including loopholes that Congress *did not* intend but that high-priced tax lawyers and accountants have found ways to create — could become untouchable once they appeared, because it would require a supermajority of the House and Senate to raise any revenue. It would become more difficult to close tax loopholes that opened up, since special-interest lobbyists could seek to block such action by preventing a supermajority in one chamber.

Finally, H.J. Res 1 would bar federal spending from exceeding 20 percent of GDP. To hit that level would require cuts of a draconian nature. This can be seen by examining the austere budget that the House of Representatives passed on April 15, sometimes referred to as the Ryan budget.

Under that budget, Medicare would be converted to a voucher system under which, the Congressional Budget Office has said, beneficiaries' out-of-pocket health-care costs would nearly triple by 2030 (relative to what those costs would be that year under the current Medicare program). CBO also has written that under the Ryan budget, federal Medicaid funding in 2030 would be 49 percent lower than it would be if the Affordable Care Act's Medicaid expansion were repealed but Medicaid otherwise was unchanged. And funding for non-security discretionary programs would be cut more than one-third below its real 2010 level. Yet CBO says that under this budget, total federal spending would be *203/4 percent of GDP in 2030*, so it would breach the allowable limit under H.J. Res 1. This illustrates the draconian nature of the proposed 20 percent-of-GDP requirement.

Another way to look at the 20 percent of GDP level is to examine federal expenditures under Ronald Reagan. Under President Reagan, who secured deep budget cuts at the start of his term, federal expenditures averaged 22 percent of GDP. And that was at a time *before* any members of the baby boom generation had retired and when health care expenditures throughout the U.S. health care system (including the private sector) were one-third lower as a share of GDP than they are today. It also was before the September 11 terrorist attacks led policymakers to create a new category of homeland security spending, and before the wars in Iraq and Afghanistan led to increases in veterans' health-care costs that will endure for a number of decades.

CONCLUSION

Policymakers need to begin to change our fiscal trajectory. As various recent commissions have indicated, we need to stabilize the debt as a share of GDP in the coming decade, and to keep it stable after that (allowing for some fluctuation over the business cycle). But establishing a balanced budget amendment in the Constitution would be most unwise. It would likely exact a heavy toll on the economy and on American businesses and workers in the years and decades ahead. It is not the course the nation should follow.

End Notes

[1] Statement of Robert D. Reischauer before the House Budget Committee, May 6, 1992.
[2] This statement was issued on January, 30, 1997.
[3] Federal Service, Transcript of Senate Budget Committee hearing, January 27, 2011.
[4] Norman Ornstein, "Four Really Dumb Ideas That Should Be Avoided," *Roll Call*, January 26, 2011.

In: Federal Budget Control
Editors: D. Groff and B. Rutherford
ISBN: 978-1- 61942-051-9

Chapter 5

STATEMENT OF ANDREW MOYLAN VICE PRESIDENT OF GOVERNMENT AFFAIRS NATIONAL TAXPAYERS UNION PREPARED FOR THE SUBCOMMITTEE ON THE CONSTITUTION COMMITTEE ON THE JUDICIARY UNITED STATES HOUSE OF REPRESENTATIVES REGARDING THE SUBCOMMITTEE'S HEARING ON WHETHER THE CONSTITUTION SHOULD BE AMENDED TO ADDRESS THE FEDERAL DEFICIT SUBMITTED MAY 13, 2011

Andrew Moylan

INTRODUCTION

Chairman Franks and distinguished Members of the Subcommittee, thank you for the opportunity to testify on behalf of the American Taxpayer regarding the important issue of a constitutional amendment to address the federal deficit. My name is Andrew Moylan, and I am Vice President of

Government Affairs for the National Taxpayers Union (NTU), a non-partisan citizen group founded in 1969 to work for lower taxes and smaller government at all levels. NTU is America's oldest non-profit grassroots taxpayer organization, with 362,000 members nationwide. We look forward to this hearing as the beginning, rather than the end, of robust and serious deliberation of constitutional protections for taxpayers, hopefully to include hearings by the full Committee on the Judiciary in this chamber and the Senate."

Few citizen groups in Washington can match NTU's decades-long history of principled advocacy in favor of a Balanced Budget Amendment (BBA), which is why I hope you will find these comments on solutions to our staggering debt problems helpful. NTU has been one of the most powerful voices in support of durable structural reforms to our budget process to protect taxpayers. We were active participants in several major campaigns to enact a B BA in Congress, including the closest-ever effort in the 104th Congress that saw House passage and fell one vote short in the Senate. During that time and to this day, NTU has additionally sought to propose a BBA for ratification through the limited amendment convention process provided under Article V of the U.S. Constitution. . You can also find further research into these topics on our website at www.ntu.org.

In pursuit of a sustainable fiscal future, NTU has worked in conjunction with friends and allies as part of the "BBA Now Coalition." The result of these deliberations is a "Common Sense Balanced Budget Amendment" proposal that has attracted the support of more than 90 grassroots and campus groups across the country. Along with NTU, our coalition includes such national groups as the American Civil Rights Union, Americans for a Balanced Budget Amendment, Americans for Tax Reform, American Solutions, Balanced Budget Amendment Now, Contract from America, Institute for Liberty, Let Freedom Ring, National Tax Limitation Committee, ReAL Action, Regular Folks United, 60 Plus Association, Tea Party Express, Young Americans for Freedom, and Young Conservatives Coalition. The proposal details and a full list of supporters can be found at the coalition's website, www.bbanow.org.

In the course of our work with coalitions such as BBA Now, other organizations, and academic experts on public finance, we have received a great deal of advice and consultation on the elements of a successful federal tax and expenditure limitation. Much of that advice and consultation has been informed by experience at the state and local level. For example, Colorado's Taxpayer's Bill of Rights (TABOR) has, since its adoption in 1992, been regarded as one of the most important constitutional mechanisms for state and local fiscal discipline ever devised. TABOR, in turn, can trace its lineage to a wealth of experience in other states. Few individuals have been as deeply involved in this process as Professor Barry Poulson of the University of Colorado. For that reason, I would like to commend Members of the Subcommittee to Professor Poulson's important work in the hopes that it might be helpful in your deliberations on a federal constitutional amendment as well as statutory mechanisms.

We were gratified that the three most important components of the BBA Now Coalition's product are reflected in several resolutions under consideration in Congress: a simple balanced budget requirement, a supermajority threshold to enact any tax increase, and a limit to prevent spending from climbing above historical averages. We believe that these three cornerstones, along with greater discipline in the appropriations process, a restructuring of our entitlement programs, and a complete overhaul of our burdensome and loophole-ridden Tax Code would provide a solid foundation for America's future.

THE PROBLEM

In the past decade, under the direction of Presidents and lawmakers from both parties, our federal budget has expanded dramatically no matter what measure one consults. At the dawn of the new millennium in 2001, federal outlays were about $1.8 trillion or 18.2 percent of our Gross Domestic Product (GDP), a level below post-World War II averages. Through the middle of the decade, we saw an explosion in spending driven by such factors as the creation of a new cabinet- level Department of Homeland Security as well as increased expenditures on defense and education. By 2003, the modest spending discipline of the late 1990s had given way to federal outlays that now seem permanently fixed at or above the post-war average of 19.6 percent of GDP. Add in the more recent surge in so-called "crisis response" spending, such as the $700 billion Troubled Asset Relief Program (TARP) of 2008 or the $862 billion "economic stimulus" bill of 2009, and the picture grows even bleaker.

In 2011, our budget is more than twice as large as in 2001, reaching about $3.8 trillion. As a percentage of our economy, 2011 outlays will surpass a level unseen since the era of full- scale war mobilization in the 1940s, at over 25 percent. Perhaps most disturbing, President Obama's estimate of our overspending problem, at roughly $1.6 trillion in 2011 is about equal, in inflation-adjusted terms, to the *entire* federal budget in 1982. Put another way, we will raise through the Tax Code and spend (in real terms) roughly the federal budget of 2003 and borrow an amount approximating the 1982 federal budget just for good measure.

Perhaps even more disturbing, Congress and Presidents alike in recent years have not only failed to grapple with our broken entitlement programs but have actually added to their size and scope. The Medicare prescription drug benefit that passed in 2003, which NTU vigorously opposed, added another layer to the program's liabilities. Just last year, the health care reform bill passed by Congress included large changes to Medicare spending that would lead to significant savings; however, that legislation spends every single dime of the savings (and more than $500 billion raised through higher taxes) on a dramatic expansion of Medicaid and a new regime of health care subsidies. These and other actions have led the nation's finances to the point where if leaders do not take corrective action soon, the United States could face a devastating debt crisis that would likely precipitate not only dramatic spending cuts but also massive tax hikes in very short order.

The federal government has seen deficits during 44 of the last 50 years. This fact ought to give pause even to die-hard Keynesians, who believe surpluses should be the norm in most economic growth cycles. While NTU's dedication to limited government would on its own lead us to conclude that this spending spree is unacceptable, sheer mathematics tell us that it is unsustainable. As of today, we are perilously close to the point where our country's debt exceeds its economic output. This sad statistic places us in rare company – just slightly below countries already staggered by debt crisis (like Ireland) and just above countries thought to be under grave threat of one (like Portugal).

THE SOLUTION

While the causes of the recent spending spree are myriad and complicated, the remedies are relatively straightforward. On the discretionary side, Congress must cancel wasteful programs, root out inefficiencies, and roll back agency spending to pre-bailout, pre-stimulus levels. With mandatory spending, Congress must take hold of the so-called "third rail" of politics with both hands and enact serious entitlement reforms primarily focused on controlling the growth in spending on Medicare and Medicaid and rectifying the terrifying prospect of Social Security operating in deficit from here on out.

Though Congress should aggressively pursue these prudent spending restraints, they will not be enough to rectify the defects of the budget process itself. Thus, Congress must enact with all deliberate speed a robust Balanced Budget Amendment to the Constitution.

As I briefly recounted earlier in this testimony, NTU's most fundamental and enduring goal has been to establish constitutional limits on the size and future growth of government. Throughout the 1970s and 1980s, my organization helped to launch and sustain the movement for a limited Article V amendment convention among the states to propose a Balanced Budget Amendment for ratification, all while pursuing a BBA through Congress. Our members were elated over the passage of S.J. Res. 58 in 1982, and the passage of H .J. Res. 1 in 1995 through the House of Representatives. In both cases the measures, whose provisions varied somewhat, fell short of enactment in the other chambers of Congress.

This history provides an illustration of how prescient the arguments of BBA advocates have proven to be, and how specious those of opponents have been. For the better part of 40 years, we were told that fiscal discipline would evolve simply by "electing the right people," all while Republican and Democratic Presidents and Congresses abused the nation's good credit. We were told that statutory measures would bring outlays under control, even as laws such as the Gramm-Rudman Hollings Act were trampled underfoot. We were told that our foundational document shouldn't be "cluttered" with mundane matters of budgeting, even as the tax-andspend culture in Washington eroded the foundations of prosperity for current and future generations.

This is particularly interesting in light of an oft-overlooked portion of our nation's history: the failure of the Articles of Confederation and the drafting of the Constitution. In 1995, NTU's then-Chairman (and current Chairman Emeritus) James Davidson testified before this very Subcommittee about that event's connection to fiscal mismanagement:

> Our Constitution was adopted precisely because of fiscal collapse under the Articles of Confederation. As Sidney Homer wrote in *A History of Interest Rates*, 'The finances of the nation were chaotic. Expenditures were authorized without the power to tax. Government credit sank so low that by 1787 certified interest-bearing claims against it were worth less than fifteen cents on the dollar. '
>
> As Sidney Homer and other historians have documented, the need to balance the budget and restore the good credit of the government led directly to the drafting of the Constitution in the first place. Mr. Homer says, 'In spite of the great potential economic strength of the new country, its financial and political system broke down completely

> in 1786. Credit at home and abroad was no longer available. The impossibility of government without money, credit, or power led to the Constitutional Convention of 1787 and a new nation in 1789.'
> It is often said that politicians do not need constitutional help to maintain fiscal responsibility; all they are supposed to need is the 'will' to do so. The evidence of our own history says otherwise. No one would argue that the great leaders who brought our country its independence lacked political will. Yet even they could not balance the budget and keep up payments on the national debt under the Articles of Confederation. It took a change in the Constitution to restore sound policy and sound credit."

The notion that limits on taxes and spending are too trivial for the Constitution seems quaint today, as our national debt tests the ominous level of 100 percent of the nation's economic output. As noted earlier, unsustainable entitlement programs, whose dire condition has been known for at least 20 years now, threaten to heap unfathomable burdens on taxpayers. BBA naysayers sought to derail the constitutional budgetary discipline that could have made adjustments to the realities of these programs gradual and bearable, all while they complained that the measure would "take too long to ratify" for it to have any salutary effect. The question now before Congress is, how could our Constitution *not* be allowed to contribute toward restoring our nation's fiscal stability? The fiscal crisis our government faces overwhelmingly demonstrates the continued relevance of a BBA to curing the maladies that threaten the health of our economy.

CURRENT PROPOSALS

To our members, a BBA would provide the very lifeblood that will restore and sustain the financial health of our Republic. We are therefore encouraged over the intensifying interest among Members of Congress and state legislators in a unified BBA concept. Several iterations of a Balanced Budget Amendment have already been introduced in the 112th Congress. NTU has traditionally supported a range of approaches to a BBA, but several merit specific discussion here.

Perhaps the most prominent proposal is the so-called "Consensus BBA" introduced by Senator Hatch (R-UT) as S.J. Res. 10 and by Representative Walsh (R-IL) as H.J. Res. 56. This resolution combines and refines elements from several amendments introduced thus far in Congress. Its structure is relatively simple. First, it directs the President to submit and Congress to enact a balanced budget while allowing for a two-thirds vote to authorize any specific excess. A two-thirds vote would also be required for any tax increase and courts would be prevented from ordering any increase in revenue. It would provide a backstop by requiring a three-fifths vote of Congress in order to approve any increase in the national debt. Further, the resolution carefully spells out how Congress could suspend the provisions of the BBA and authorize specific additional spending to address national security threats: by majority vote in the event of a declared war, and by three-fifths vote in any other type of military conflict. Finally, it enacts a spending limitation that will hold federal spending to 18 percent of GDP.

NTU supports this proposal for its strength and comprehensiveness and its proper focus on the true cause of our fiscal maladies: overspending. By including a strong expenditure limitation, this version of a BBA would provide a vital check on irresponsible budgeting. Although several types of mechanisms could answer to the purpose of controlling growth in expenditures, any such protection incorporating Gross Domestic Product must pay careful heed to historical experience. In this case, NTU believes that an annual spending cap at 18 percent of GDP is clearly the most prudent choice. Such a level reflects the share of economic output that federal revenues have typically represented since World War II. Given that constitutional amendments should be designed with a long nod to the past and an equally farsighted view to the future, 18 percent is a most stable and logical benchmark.

In addition, setting the expenditure limit at 18 percent would make a valuable contribution toward harmonizing all parts of the amendment so that the whole functions as intended. An assumption that spending should normally be linked to the average and customary federal revenue proportion would, by its very nature, give Congress and the President a starting point that is closer to balance. Indeed, the limit helps to remedy Washington's increasingly metastasized affliction of tax-spend-and-borrow, by elevating the concept of expenditure restraint to its rightful place in policymaking. While the two-thirds "supermajority" override requirement is essential to ensuring this place, so is the 18 percent cap on expenditures. If set too high, the spending limit would merely institutionalize, rather than minimize, deficits. Recent spending-to-GDP ratios in excess of 20 percent – and the resulting pressures to borrow or tax even more – ought to convince fiscal disciplinarians of the need for a carefully-designed limit, given that Washington has only collected more than 20 percent of GDP in revenues three times since 1940.

Another strong BBA proposal is S.J. Res. 5, introduced by Senator Mike Lee (R-UT). This version is similar in structure to the aforementioned "Consensus BBA," with a balanced budget requirement, an 18 percent spending cap, and a supermajority threshold for tax hikes but is stricter in several areas. First, it harmonizes all supermajority requirements at a two-thirds vote of Congress. Second, it contains no specific language authorizing excesses for national security purposes, preferring to allow the supermajority override option to serve that purpose.

Senators Cornyn (R-TX) and Hatch (R-UT) have also introduced a BBA, S.J. Res. 3, which would achieve many of the same goals, though its spending limit is placed at a higher level of 20 percent of GDP, roughly the historical post-war average for outlays. In your chamber, Representative Bob Goodlatte (R-VA) has continued his long history of leadership on this issue by introducing H.J. Res. 1, which incorporates other supermajority requirements and spending limitations, and H.J. Res. 2, which takes a more basic stance. All of these proposals, and perhaps some others yet to be introduced, deserve consideration, but Congress must do so without delay.

In NTU's opinion some particular BBA concepts are worthy of further deliberation, and some should be avoided. While many proposals in Congress achieve a cap on spending by limiting it to a certain percentage of GDP, this is not the only way to achieve such a goal. Basing a limitation on a prior year's revenues, or receipts over a range of years, could achieve similar aims. However, we would strongly urge Members to avoid any provisions to exempt certain portions of the federal budget from a BBA. This policy would provide an enormous loophole through which to drive additional spending and unleash a destructive lobbying war over what programs should receive special status.

Rebuttals to Common Arguments against a BBA

The latter, chilling prospect aside, a legion of BBA opponents has for quite some time waged war against the very notion of a constitutional protection against greater debt. Some of the arguments they deploy have gained an unwarranted amount of political currency and I'd like to address the more common ones here.

During the BBA debates of the 1980s and 1990s, one familiar refrain from opponents was that an amendment was simply unnecessary to restrain deficits because Congress could do so on its own. If political "will" were enough to protect citizens from unwise or pernicious legislation, then we could likewise do without the all-important First Amendment to the Constitution as well since Congress could simply refrain from passing any laws abridging freedom of speech. But our Founders recognized, and citizens and scholars now universally accept, the need for limitations on the power of government to abridge fundamental rights such as these. So it is that we must limit the power of legislators to imperil our nation's finances and our children's future. Just as our Founders did, Congresses and Presidents both present and future need a credible fiscal structure and reasonable guidelines within which they can operate. A strong BBA would provide exactly that kind of protection. Though prominent in prior debates, this argument ought to have no relevance now that we've had decades of intervening experience with scarcely interrupted (and bipartisan) support for ever-higher debt to the detriment of our fiscal health.

The common refrain heard today is that a BBA would be a "depression-maker" because it would prevent Congress from utilizing fiscal policy to counteract an economic recession. The response to this contention is two-fold: one technical, the other practical. The technical response is that under the "Consensus BBA," Congress can enact whatever kind of spending or tax policies it likes so long as two-thirds of its Members vote in the affirmative. Other proposals include lower thresholds, such as three-fifths, to achieve such an override. These provisions preserve Congressional flexibility by allowing large majorities to act in times of emergency.

The practical response is that despite claims to the contrary, Congress is not only capable of achieving such supermajorities but has done so regularly when faced with truly urgent decision points in recent history. For example, when the financial panic of late 2008 gripped the nation, Congress passed the Troubled Asset Relief Program with strong bipartisan supermajorities in both chambers (including 74 votes in the Senate). Setting aside for a moment whether or not TARP was good policy (for the record, NTU was a staunch opponent), it was clearly advertised as an emergency measure to prevent an economic collapse. For better or worse, Congress took that advice and passed the bill with votes from both parties.

For further evidence, we can look to supplemental appropriations bills. In recent years, these have generally fallen into two categories: spending on wars, or response to natural disasters. Disaster spending tends to draw strong support and pass with huge majorities, but the vigorous public debate surrounding the wars in Iraq and Afghanistan led to much closer votes. NTU took no position on U.S. involvement in these conflicts, but it is clear that policies enjoying widespread public support have no trouble clearing a supermajority hurdle while policies that are controversial have a more uncertain path.

Some opponents of a BBA contend that we have never enshrined any specific economic policy in the Constitution and should not do so now. But the BBA is not an economic policy and it is not a federal budget; it is a set of guidelines within which Congress can create economic policy and a federal budget. It is no more an economic policy than the 21st Amendment, which repealed alcohol prohibition, was a specific regulatory policy for states. Neither of these amendments prescribes the manner in which legislators must incorporate them in daily policy; they simply lay out the ground rules for the debate.

Others argue that a BBA would take too much time and effort to ratify and gain the force of law. While it is true that ratification can be protracted, the process of amending our Constitution is rightly one that involves meeting strict criteria. Nonetheless, the obvious point needs to be made: had the Senate followed the House's lead in 1995 and passed the BBA, the measure could very well have been ratified and operating for the better part of a decade by now. In any case, NTU urges passage of statutory language in pursuit of the same goals expressed in a Balanced Budget Amendment to help bridge the gap. Still, given that statutory measures exist at the whim of Congress, taxpayers can only count on a strong constitutional measure to protect them from fiscal disaster.

There are often questions about how such an amendment would be enforced. Some say that a B BA is essentially unenforceable because there is nothing that will compel Congress to comply with its mandates, but that cynical view could be extended to virtually any policy, whether constitutional or statutory. President Jackson famously said of an 1832 Supreme Court decision, "[Chief Justice] John Marshall has made his decision, now let him enforce it!" Marshall, of course, did not have an army at his disposal and could rely only upon the tensile strength of the fabric of our system of checks and balances and robust public involvement in the federal government. As with essentially every other policy, a BBA would be enforced through these tools if a violation occurred.

BBA opponents argue that it is unwise for it to include a spending limitation since that would necessitate large reductions in expenditures over the coming years. First, it is simply not accurate to characterize a return of spending to post-war revenue averages as any kind of "steep" or "draconian" cut. Further, even the most aggressive budget outline that has been proposed (by the Republican Study Committee, the caucus of House conservatives) would envision outlays hovering around $3.3 trillion (an amount just shy of 2009 expenditures of $3.5 trillion) and then modestly increasing to $4.3

trillion by the end of the decade. This would merely allow for the historical trend for spending increases to catch up with the massive spikes witnessed in 2009 and 2010. But most importantly, these kinds of reductions are absolutely necessary to changing our trajectory of ever-increasing deficits and debt. We must begin to reduce spending now to ward off fiscal catastrophe.

Others argue that a BBA in and of itself does nothing to solve the long-term drivers of our debt: entitlement costs. While technically correct, no single policy is likely to solve those problems and the Constitution would be the wrong place to deal with such details. What a BBA will do is ensure that future leaders do not dig the debt hole any further and that that they do not habitually deviate from historical norms on spending. By establishing those boundaries, the BBA will give Congress the proper incentives to finally grapple with entitlement reform,

CONCLUSION

Thomas Jefferson, a hero to many conservatives, once wrote, "I wish it were possible to obtain a single amendment to our Constitution ...; I mean an additional article, taking from the federal government the power of borrowing." Franklin D. Roosevelt, a hero to many liberals, once said, "Let us have the courage to stop borrowing to meet continuing deficits. Revenues must cover expenditures by one means or another. Any government, like any family, can, for a year, spend a little more than it earns. But you and I know that a continuation of that habit means the poorhouse." Though they lived more than a century apart in time and miles apart on the ideological spectrum, both of these titans of American history recognized the threat posed by deficits and expressed support for policies to make them a thing of the past.

No proposal in Congress today would guarantee such an outcome – an end to deficit spending. What a BBA will guarantee is a more deliberative, accountable budgeting process that avoids the rash impulse to tax or borrow and encourages consensus-building toward spending restraint. Constitutions shouldn't make policy, but they should set rules within which policymakers operate and they should safeguard the rights of citizens. If the fundamental right – of every generation – to be free of excessive federal debt cannot be protected by our Constitution, little else in that precious document will matter. Thus, the past, present, and future all speak clearly to us on behalf of this reform.

In: Federal Budget Control
Editors: D. Groff and B. Rutherford
ISBN: 978-1- 61942-051-9

Chapter 6

STATUTORY LIMITS ON TOTAL SPENDING AS A METHOD OF BUDGET CONTROL

Megan Suzanne Lynch

SUMMARY

Often when there is dissatisfaction with budgetary levels, budget process reforms are proposed to mandate a specific budgetary policy or fiscal objective. This report focuses specifically on one such budget process reform—the concept of creating a statutory limit on total spending.

As discussed in this report, a total spending limit consists of statutory long-term or permanent limits on federal spending coupled with a statutory enforcement mechanism that would make automatic reductions in spending in the event that compliance with the limits is not achieved through legislative action. Such spending limits would comprise any new spending as well as spending that results from previously enacted law. By encompassing all types of spending, and by including a statutory enforcement mechanism, a total spending limit attempts to remedy a perceived limitation of the congressional budget resolution, under which Congress establishes limits on spending in various categories that can be enforced or waived by Congress at its own discretion.

The recent growth in spending, both in dollar terms and relative to the economy, has generated support for total limits on spending. Several groups and organizations have recommended a total spending cap, and on July 19,

2011, the House passed H.R. 2560, the Cut, Cap and Balance Act of 2011, which includes total spending limits for FY2013 through FY2021. In addition, the House-passed budget resolution for FY2012, H.Con.Res. 34, includes a policy statement calling for Congress to enact total spending limits. Other legislative proposals introduced in the 112th Congress include total spending limits, such as S. 245, H.R. 1605, H.R. 1848, and H.R. 2041.

The potential effectiveness of a statutory limit on total spending is complicated by projection uncertainty, unforeseen events, and especially the complex nature of direct spending. Statutory limits have been subject to criticism for ceding Congress's "power of the purse," targeting spending rather than the deficit or debt, attempting to address a budgetary problem through procedure instead of policy changes that would themselves reduce spending, and for other reasons.

This report provides information on the concept of a statutory limit on total spending, including objectives, complications, and criticisms. The report also includes information on the many features of spending limit proposals, which can vary considerably. Lastly, the report provides observations on budgetary controls, similar to statutory spending limits, from an historical perspective.

INTRODUCTION

An array of budget process reform proposals are put forth each year seeking to refine or improve the existing constitutional requirements, laws, and rules that make up the federal budget process.[1] Some proposals are designed not only to modify the budget process, but also to produce specific budgetary outcomes. Particularly popular when there is dissatisfaction with debt or deficit levels, such proposals seek to establish a legal mandate for a budgetary policy or fiscal objective, such as a specific limit on the deficit level, or the requirement for a balanced federal budget. This report focuses specifically on one such budget process reform: the concept of creating a statutory limit on total spending.

A total spending limit, often referred to as an overall spending cap or an omnicap,[2] consists of statutory long-term or permanent limits on federal spending, encompassing both discretionary and direct spending (also referred to as mandatory or entitlement spending).[3] Further, the analysis in this report concerns measures that propose a total spending limit that also include an automatic statutory mechanism to enforce the spending limit in the event that compliance is not achieved through legislative action. This form of cap should be distinguished from other mechanisms that may limit spending, but do not include an automatic means to enforce the specified levels. For example, this report excludes proposals to create total spending limits that are enforced only by points of order, or proposals to institute a constitutional amendment requiring a balanced budget, which generally lack any automatic enforcement mechanism.[4]

Generally, total spending limits would operate by first establishing in statute a specific total spending limit for each year. At some point during each year, Congress would be informed of a projected overall spending total and the amount, if any, by which the statutory spending limit is projected to be breached. After a period of time, during which Congress would presumably attempt to achieve compliance with the spending limits through legislative action, a final determination would be made as to whether the spending limit had been breached. In the event of a breach, an automatic enforcement mechanism would impose reductions in spending. As with many features of the proposals, the proposed enforcement mechanisms could vary significantly. They may include exemptions for specific programs, as well as provide for suspension of enforcement under specific circumstances, such as war.

The recent growth in spending, both in dollar terms and relative to the economy as a whole, has garnered support for total limits on spending. Several groups and organizations have recommended a total spending cap, though few provide detail on what such a legislative proposal might include. Some legislative proposals have been introduced in the 112th Congress, however, such as S. 245, introduced by Senator Bob Corker, and a companion measure, H.R. 1605 introduced by Representative John J. Duncan Jr.; H.R. 1848, introduced by Representative Connie Mack; H.R. 2041, introduced by Representative Jack Kingston; and H.R. 2560, introduced by Representative Jason Chaffetz.[5] In addition, the House-passed budget resolution for FY2012, H.Con.Res. 34, includes a policy statement on budget enforcement that calls for Congress to enact total spending limits, and on July 19, 2011, the House passed H.R. 2560, which includes total spending limits for FY2013-FY2021.

The following sections provide a general discussion of the objectives, challenges, and criticisms of total spending limits. The next section of the report discusses typical features of total spending limits and provides information on how they may vary. The final section of the report includes observations on compliance with the spending limits, based on historical experiences with statutory budget controls.

INTENDED OBJECTIVES AND ADVANTAGES

The main objective of total spending limits appears to be to acknowledge and address a recent growth in federal spending. In FY2000, total federal outlays equaled 18.2% of gross domestic product (GDP). By FY2010, total federal outlays reached 23.8% of GDP. Under the CBO baseline, totals outlays are projected to reach 24.0% of GDP in FY2021 under current policy.[6]

Further, overall spending limits apparently intend to address the growing deficit and debt levels. Concern has grown over an increasing deficit and its potential effect on the nation's fiscal and economic health. The budget deficit each year from 2009 to 2011 has been the highest ever in dollar terms and significantly higher as a share of GDP than in any other year since World War II. The budget is not projected to be on a sustainable path under current policy, in the sense that the federal debt will continue to grow more quickly than GDP. Although there has been no difficulty financing the deficit to date, at some point, investors could refuse to continue to finance deficits that they believed were unsustainable.[7]

Although some lawmakers advocate a combination of spending decreases and revenue increases to address the deficit, proponents of total spending limit proposals have often been associated with the belief that all or much of deficit reduction policy should take place through decreases in spending. Although a spending limit could theoretically be combined with revenue increases, current proponents of spending limits typically seek to assure that reductions in spending be primarily used to confront the growing deficit.

There are additional objectives underlying the concept of statutory spending limits, which is particularly noticeable because the congressional budget resolution already exists as a method of setting and enforcing desired spending levels.[8] Statutory limits on total spending address at least two perceived limitations of the congressional budget resolution.

First, the levels in the congressional budget resolution are generally enforced by raising points of order on the House and Senate floor against provisions in budgetary legislation. Such an enforcement mechanism relies on Members affirmatively raising points of order against the legislation, and most of these points of order can be waived by a majority or super-majority of each chamber. Further, points of order can limit spending only in new legislation being considered by Congress; they cannot limit spending that results from previously enacted legislation, from which more than half of current spending arises.[9] Total spending limits would establish a more stringent enforcement mechanism, one that would be automatically triggered to make cuts to already enacted spending, and could only be waived though the enactment of further legislation. This could possibly overcome what some perceive as institutional barriers to cutting spending. For example, although many lawmakers may favor decreases in spending, reaching legislative agreement on which programs specifically should be cut is difficult, both procedurally and politically. An automatic reduction mechanism would tend to ensure the occurrence of spending cuts, even without legislative agreement.

Second, although the congressional budget resolution sets a desired level of overall spending for a specific year, the budget resolution is not required to adherence to any specific budgetary policy. Further, Congress is not required to maintain any specific spending levels from one annual budget resolution to the next. The same is true for the President's annual budget submission. Further, no alignment is required between the spending levels proposed in the President's budget submission and those established by the congressional budget resolution. Statutory limits on total spending would establish a federal budgetary policy which would likely require that the spending levels in the President's budget proposal and the congressional budget resolution align. Alleviating future controversy over appropriate levels of overall annual spending may facilitate the development and agreement on substantive policy changes to achieve the spending limits. Furthermore, setting total spending caps would establish a federal budgetary policy that remains consistent year after year, despite changes in the presidency or Congress.

CHALLENGES AND COMPLICATIONS

The implementation of any overall spending limit may raise difficulties stemming from several causes. First, as mentioned above, the levels of spending stipulated under any cap would presumably have to be established on the basis of economic and fiscal projections that inherently involve some uncertainty. The level of spending may also be affected by unforeseen events that budgetary projections cannot take into account even through estimates. Finally, levels of direct spending are especially subject to unpredictable variations.

Using projections as a basis for budgetary decisions can be problematic because they are highly sensitive to small changes in underlying assumptions and economic factors and are subject to substantial margins of error, even over short periods of time. Based on history, actual outcomes can be much better or worse than projections. The Office of Management and Budget (OMB) estimates that the absolute average errors for its budget deficit projections are 1.5% of GDP for the next budget year and 3.5% of GDP for five years in the future.[10] Making programmatic changes to achieve fiscal goals based on these projections, therefore, must be expected to result in changes that ultimately over- or under-shoot what is intended. Furthermore, as described below, under certain circumstances, the need to base estimates on projections may make it possible to generate projections that conform to stipulated targets by appropriate adjustment of the assumptions underlying the projections.

Unforeseen events present a dimension of uncertainty that goes beyond what is inherent to trends in current fiscal and economic activity. Many of the legislative spending increases that occurred in the past decade were due to events that could reasonably regarded as extraordinary or unforeseen, including the terrorist attacks of September 11, 2001, ongoing military operations in Afghanistan and Iraq, Hurricane Katrina and other natural disasters, and the 2008 financial crisis. Creating statutory spending caps may limit Congress's flexibility in responding to future unforeseen events, whether they be natural disasters or situations that Members conclude require increased domestic, defense, or international spending. As described below, some proposals include mechanisms such as waivers or emergency exemptions to deal with such unanticipated events as they occur, although it could be argued that creating such an exemption mechanism risks compromising the overall goals of statutory spending caps.

One of the most intricate complications that overall spending targets must address would arise from their inclusion of direct as well as discretionary spending. Total spending for direct spending programs, which currently makes up over half of total federal spending and is forecast to grow rapidly in the future, is difficult to control or limit for several reasons. First, unlike discretionary spending programs, which are funded through annual appropriations, direct spending programs generally are not controlled through annual appropriations actions, but are instead controlled through other permanent or multi-year laws, meaning that most will automatically continue to operate each year, barring congressional action to the contrary.

Second, direct spending legislation typically results from the establishment of a program that includes eligibility or benefit criteria and a payment formula that together dictate the overall amount the program will spend. The levels of spending resulting from these over any future period can be ascertained only as a projection; in addition, however, the effect on future spending of any policy changes in the program can be estimated in advance only on the basis of assumptions about the effects of the changes themselves.

If levels of direct spending are projected to be higher than desired, eligibility criteria or payment formulas must be altered to attempt to achieve the desired funding level. This means that under current circumstances, to affect direct spending, Congress has to choose to develop, consider, and adopt a measure that would adjust eligibility criteria or payment formulas with the hope that the changes would cause direct spending to fall to a desired level.

Accurately predicting the budgetary effect of a policy change on direct spending levels is also difficult. A survey and report by the Government Accountability Office (GAO), titled *Issues in Capping Mandatory Spending*, discusses some of the complicating characteristics of direct spending programs that make achieving a specific spending level very difficult.[11] For example, changing eligibility criteria to eliminate a group of individuals may result in large savings or no savings, depending on how many services those individuals typically use. Also, the use of non-cash benefits makes it difficult to predict costs and savings because eliminating some services, such as nursing home care, could shift demand to other high-cost services, like impatient hospitalization.

All these uncertainties create challenges for Congress in trying to enact legislation that would achieve a desired level of funding. They can also complicate how an enforcement mechanism, such as sequestration, would work. If a direct spending program required an automatic reduction, for example, of 4%, how that might be implemented is not clear. Determining what policy changes to direct spending programs would be necessary to save a specified amount of money could prove very difficult.

CRITICISMS

Criticisms that have been raised of spending limit proposals have rested on several grounds. Some criticisms apply specifically to limits on total spending, and some apply to any proposal to amend the current budget process in a way that seeks to force future action.

For example, some have argued that past budgetary limits enforced by automatic reductions led Congress to accept "second- or even third-best solutions" to problems in an effort to stay within its short-term budget constraints.[12] It has also been suggested that such processes have heightened conflict within Congress, as well as between Congress and the President.[13] Lastly, it can be argued that relying on automatic reductions to fulfill budgetary levels cedes Congress's control over levels and details of spending.

Spending limit proposals may be subject to the criticism that they may not automatically translate into reductions in the debt or the deficit. While the controls on spending that are associated with spending limits may be viewed as having an inherent tendency also to reduce the deficit or debt, it could be argued that they may not necessarily have this effect, to the extent that they fail to take into account revenue levels as well. For example, even if Congress adheres to specific spending limits that would be projected to bring the budget into balance, if it simultaneously reduces revenue, or if revenue falls due to economic conditions, a deficit may still exist, or even increase. Deficits may be particularly sensitive to this latter concern because the economic conditions that would tend to produce an upsurge in spending for programs such as Medicaid and the Supplemental Nutrition Program (SNAP) would also tend to reduce revenues. Further, capping spending would not reduce the debt currently held by the public unless spending levels were lower than revenue levels, resulting in a surplus that could be used to pay down such debt.[14]

In addition, some argue that to address a deficit or debt problem, both spending decreases and revenue increases must occur, and this means including revenue increases as part of an enforcement mechanism.[15] This argument may reflect an implicit presumption that, whether addressed in policy or in an enforcement mechanism, the spending cuts that would be required to bring the deficit down to sustainable levels would be too severe to be palatable and therefore, a combination of changes to spending and revenue would be required.

It has been argued that placing a cap on total spending with no parallel limits on revenue decreases would encourage "the conversion of spending programs into tax expenditures, which would not count against the cap," favoring subsidies provided through the tax code.[16] Some further assert that this approach would encourage tax expenditures that would tend to favor high-income households and corporations over types of government assistance that benefit primarily low- and middle-income populations because the former have greater tax liability on average than the latter.[17] As a result, in addition, such a shift in emphasis of policy mechanisms may result in the deficit either staying the same, or potentially growing.

Another criticism of spending limit proposals is that they seek to achieve a budgetary goal through procedure, rather than directly through proposing policy that would achieve the stated spending goal. When discussing such budget process reforms, a sentiment exists among some that is reflected in the often repeated saying "the process is not the problem; the problem is the problem."[18] According to this argument, process reform is being suggested as a substitute for, or distraction from, the tough policy decisions that are needed to actually address the budgetary problem.

From this perspective, the major obstacle to reducing spending could be viewed as a lack of consensus and political will, and the creation of statutory spending targets could be considered as not, in itself, addressing either of these elements. It has been argued that budget process reforms, such as spending limits, are best implemented when accompanied by a policy package that achieves a corresponding purpose. For example, the Balanced Budget and Emergency Deficit Control Act of 1985, referred to as the Gramm-Rudman-Hollings Act, created statutory annual deficit targets. Many question the act's success and some attribute a lack of success to the fact that no spending reductions or revenue increases were included because agreement on such changes could not be reached.[19] Conversely, the Budget Enforcement Act of 1990, which created statutory discretionary spending limits and PAYGO, is considered by many to have been successful, in part because these mechanisms were included as part of a reconciliation bill that itself significantly reduced the deficit. The procedures were used to enforce the savings achieved through changes in spending and revenue policy, instead of acting as a substitute for them. As a former CBO director concluded, budget process mechanisms are better at enforcing agreements than forcing agreements.[20]

FEATURES AND OPTIONS

Amount and Coverage

Proposals for a total cap on spending specify an actual spending limit or amount, which may appear in different forms, some seeking to cap or freeze spending at a specific rate, others trying to reduce spending annually. Although such limits could be represented as a static dollar amount, most proposals include spending limits that are linked to some other economic or demographic factors such as GDP, inflation, or population growth. For example, S. 245 stipulates that outlays for FY2014 through FY2022, be 25% of GDP minus 0.1711% in each successive fiscal year (i.e., 24.8289 % in FY2014 and 23.4601 % in FY2022). H.R. 2560 specifies that outlays may not exceed 21.7% of GDP in FY2013, with decreasing GDP limits for each year until FY2021. H.R. 4529 (111th Congress) also would have limited spending to a percentage of GDP, though the percentage fluctuates between 21.6% and

24.1% from FY2011 to FY2037 before steadily decreasing through FY2083 to 13.0%.

Recommendations have been made by some outside Congress to cap total spending at a rate that allows increases at the inflation rate plus population growth[21] or to establish a limit that allows spending to grow at the inflation rate minus 1%.[22] H.R. 5323 (111th Congress) would have prohibited spending from increasing at a rate greater than the percentage change in the Consumer Price Index plus the percentage change in annual population growth. Although these measures may appear to allow spending to increase, because spending rises in dollar terms, they likely represent a decrease compared with current policy, as measured by the CBO baseline.

Spending limits vary not just by type, but also by severity and pace of reduction. The spending limits in the proposals described above range from 24.8289% to 13% of GDP. To put that into perspective, total spending as a percentage of GDP was 23.8% in FY2010 and 25.0% in FY2009.

As a share of GDP, these were the highest levels of spending since 1946. From 1946 to 2008, spending averaged 19.6% of GDP. The proposed level of 13% in FY2083 provided in H.R. 4529 (111th Congress) would have been the lowest level of federal spending since 1941.

Projected Versus Actual Levels

Proposals for spending limits also differ in whether they define their standards for compliance in terms of projected or actual levels of annual spending or any other quantities referenced in the proposals, such as GDP or population growth. The choice of standards is especially important in relation to a cap that covers total spending because it will encompass direct spending which is more challenging to project than discretionary spending. If a proposal relies on spending projections (rather than actual levels), then at some point, typically near the beginning of the calendar year, a projection of total spending must be made. In this situation, Congress might then pass legislation making adjustments sufficient to eliminate the difference between projected spending and the statutory limit. In this situation, the success of Congress in adhering to the spending limits will be determined solely on the basis of whether Congress enacts spending reductions that are projected to be adequate to meet the spending limits. As a result, however, if the projections later prove inaccurate Congress will not have technically adhered to the spending limits, but appropriate amounts of actual spending reduction may not have taken place.

On the other hand, if a proposal plans to rely on actual levels of spending to enforce the limits, and Congress makes legislative adjustments to spending law based on projections of spending levels made at the beginning of the year, but actual spending later turns out to be higher than was projected, Congress will not have met the levels through no fault of its own and the enforcement mechanism may be implemented. This situation also presents a challenge to implementing the enforcement mechanism, because the spending will already have taken place. In this case, therefore, success in meeting the targets relies not just on congressional action but also on the accuracy of the projections.

Some have suggested incorporating a mechanism, referred to as a "look back" provision, that might rely on both projected and actual levels when measuring compliance with the spending limit. In such a scenario, success in meeting the spending limit would be based initially on the ability to meet projected spending levels. If subsequently, however, the actual level of spending for that period is shown to be significantly higher than was projected, it may require some type of automatic reduction to occur.[23]

Exemptions and Waivers from the Total Spending Limits

Exemptions and waivers appear in many proposals to create total spending caps as a way to grant Congress flexibility in making budgetary decisions. Exemptions provide certain programs with protection, and waivers allow Congress flexibility for dealing with future circumstances. As described in the following section, proposals may specify that certain programs are exempt from the automatic enforcement mechanism in the event that it is triggered.

Some proposals exempt certain spending from counting against the prescribed limit. For instance, some proposals exempt from the overall cap funds being used to pay interest or principal on the national debt. Others, such as S. 245, and H.R. 5323 (111th Congress), would direct that spending identified as "emergency" not count against the limits. Especially in the latter case, exemptions create the potential for significant spending to occur that is not subject to the limits, particularly because Congress decides what constitutes emergency spending.

In addition to exemptions, proposals may provide for waivers that have the effect of setting aside the spending limits and any related enforcement mechanism under specified circumstances. In the case of points of order on the House or Senate floor, most proposals set forth a mechanism for either chamber to waive those points of order if it wishes to do so, sometimes requiring a super-majority of the chamber. For example, S. 245 states that points of order can be waived in the Senate by an affirmative vote of two-thirds of the Senators, present and voting, and in the House by adoption of a special rule[24] requiring an affirmative vote of two-thirds of the Members, present and voting.

Proposals often provide for a method of waiving or suspending the overall spending limits in specific situations. For instance, proposals have permitted waivers if the United States is engaged in war or if the United States is experiencing difficult economic conditions, such as low economic growth. Past use of sequestration allowed such flexibility. For instance, suspension in the event of a recession was provided in past statutory budget controls, such as the Balanced Budget and Emergency Deficit Control Act of 1985, often referred to as the Gramm-Rudman-Hollings Act.[25] This act created statutory deficit targets that were enforced by an automatic reduction mechanism, referred to as sequestration. Under the Gramm-Rudman-Hollings Act, if a recession occurred, Congress could consider a joint resolution, under expedited procedures, that once enacted would suspend the deficit reduction provisions for the current fiscal year or for all fiscal years.[26]

Proposals could also explicitly allow for the Congress to suspend the limits and any resulting automatic reduction at its discretion. For example, the Balanced Budget and Emergency Deficit Control Reaffirmation Act of 1987 (P.L. 100-119) provided for the consideration of a joint resolution suspending sequestration, to be considered under expedited procedures if introduced by the House or Senate majority leader within 10 days of receipt of OMB's sequestration report. Similarly, H.R. 4529 (111th Congress) included a section providing for the consideration of a joint resolution directing the President to modify the sequestration order, to be considered under expedited procedures if introduced by either the House or Senate majority leader after the sequester order but before the end of the relevant session of Congress.

Enforcement

As mentioned above, total spending limits, as discussed in this report, include only those that establish an automatic mechanism to enforce the spending limit in the event that it is not achieved through legislation. Automatic enforcement would occur after the fact, if congressional action failed to achieve the target levels of spending, typically through a process of automatic reduction. Some proposals may also establish means by which spending limits can be enforced in advance of the enactment of spending legislation, typically through points of order raised during consideration of such legislation in each house. This section discusses both types of enforcement mechanism.

Points of Order

The chief form of enforcement mechanism operating in advance of the enactment of spending legislation is points of order that can be raised on the House and Senate floor against legislation that would violate the statutory spending limits. For example, a proposal may include language providing that it is not in order to consider in the House or Senate any measure that would cause applicable spending limits to be exceeded. Because such rules are not self enforcing, such an enforcement mechanism relies on Members affirmatively raising points of order on the House or Senate floor against the legislation. It should be noted that, unless specified in the proposal, in most cases, points of order can be waived. When the House chooses to waive points of order, it typically does so through a special rule reported from the House Rules Committee and adopted by the House, although it may also do so through the suspension of the rules procedure or by unanimous consent. Many rules related to the budget process allow three-fifths of all Senators (60 if there is no more than one vacancy) to agree to a motion to waive the point of order. Similarly, spending limit proposals may seek to make it more difficult to waive points of order by requiring a super majority, such as two-thirds or three-fifths of the chamber to agree.

Both the reliance of points of order on elective action by Members and their potential for being waived has often led to their being criticized as a weak form of enforcement mechanism. Their most significant limitation in this context, however, is that they can only apply to new spending legislation when it is being considered by Congress. Points of order can never limit spending resulting from previously enacted legislation, which includes most direct spending and makes up about 55% of total spending.

With the exception of Statutory PAYGO,[27] all mechanisms currently used in the congressional budget process to enforce spending levels rely solely on points of order. For example, spending levels in the budget resolution are generally enforced through points of order, again meaning that they can only affect new legislation.[28] In part, the automatic enforcement mechanisms that are a component of proposals to create total spending limits represent a response to the limitations of point of order as an enforcement mechanism.

Automatic Reduction Mechanism (Sequestration)

The purpose of including automatic enforcement mechanisms in proposals to create total spending limits is to enforce spending limits on spending that results from already enacted legislation. These mechanisms are designed to make automatic cuts to spending programs when total spending limits are breached.

Although this would need to be specified in statute, in a general sense, the automatic reductions would be achieved by the President issuing an order that would automatically implement programmatic spending cuts to compensate for the level by which the spending caps have been breached. These cuts are often referred to as across-the-board cuts, although as explained below, they often include exemptions that protect specified programs.

Such automatic spending reductions have existed as an enforcement mechanism in several forms in connection with budget and budget process reform, each time referred to as sequestration. Sequestration is currently used to enforce Statutory PAYGO. Before that, it was included in the Gramm-Rudman-Hollings Act and the Balanced Budget and Emergency Deficit Control Reaffirmation Act of 1987 to enforce annually declining deficit targets. It was also used in the Budget Enforcement Act of 1990[29] and the Budget Enforcement Act of 1997[30] to enforce discretionary spending limits and PAYGO.

Sequestration is included as an enforcement mechanism in many proposals, such as S. 245 and H.R. 2560 (112th Congress) and H.R. 4529 and H.R. 5323 (111th Congress). For example, S. 245 states that not later than 45 calendar days after the beginning of a fiscal year, the OMB shall conduct a sequestration to eliminate any excess outlay amount.

Exemptions and Limitations from the Automatic Reduction Mechanism

Automatic reduction mechanisms can be tailored to shield specified programs, meaning certain programs might be completely exempt from across the board cuts, or they might be protected by a limit on the percentage of cut to which a program can be subject. For example, under Statutory PAYGO, some direct spending programs and activities are exempt from sequestration, such as Social Security and Tier I Railroad Retirement benefits, federal employee retirement and disability programs, Supplemental Security Income (SSI), Supplemental Nutrition Assistance Program (SNAP), Children's Health Insurance Program (CHIP), Temporary Assistance for Needy Families (TANF), veterans' programs, net interest, refundable income tax credits,

Medicaid, and unemployment compensation. In 2010, these exemptions amounted to roughly half of total federal spending.

Some spending limit proposals create similar protections. For example, H.R. 4529 (111th Congress) would have exempted from reduction payments for net interest, Social Security benefits in certain circumstances, certain veterans benefits, obligated balances of budget authority carried over from prior years, any obligation of the federal government required to be paid under the U.S. Constitution, any program whose growth in the budget year is equal to or less than the consumer price index, and intergovernmental transfers.

Similarly, sequestration can be tailored to provide a more limited shield for non-exempt programs. For example, under Gramm-Rudman-Hollings, sequestration could reduce spending for certain programs only by 1% in 1986 and 2% in subsequent years. These programs were Medicare, veterans' medical care, community health centers, migrant health centers, and Indian health facilities and services. For other programs, such as guaranteed student loans and child support enforcement, specific rules governed the calculation of sequestration reductions.

Exempting certain programs means that non-exempt programs would need to be cut by larger amounts to achieve the desired reduction in overall spending. Senate Finance Committee Chairman Senator Max Baucus asserted, in a statement on automatic enforcement mechanisms, "If Medicare, Medicaid and Social Security were exempted from an across-the-board-cut, the cuts to other programs would be far too large to bear."[31]

Level of Reduction Made by the Automatic Reduction Mechanism

Many proposals direct that the amount by which spending is reduced through the automatic reduction mechanism must be the amount by which the spending limit is breached. Proposals, however, could include limits to the amount that could be cut by the reduction mechanism.

For example, H.R. 4529 (111th Congress) stated that if spending limits are not met, a sequestration will occur making cuts to all non-exempt spending programs. The proposal, however, included a provision stating that "No program shall be subject to a spending reduction of more than one percent of its budgetary resources."

Similarly, S. 245 provides that if spending limits are not met, an across the board cut would apply to all programs within each of three specified categories in proportion to the growth in outlays in such category over the previous year. Under such an arrangement, spending can be cut only to an amount tied to the actual growth in the category to which it belongs. As a result, the maximum reduction that could be achieved through a sequester would reduce overall spending to the level of the previous year.

Application to Different Categories of Spending

Some proposals may allow for cuts under sequestration to apply differently to different categories of spending. For example, Gramm-Rudman-Hollings included general deficit targets that were enforced by sequestration with spending reductions equally divided between defense and non-defense programs, but with most direct spending programs either exempt from cuts or protected from receiving a reduction of more than 1% or 2%. In some cases, however, Congress acted to reduce discretionary spending, but deficit targets were still not achieved, because of the impact of revenues and direct spending. As a result, automatic reductions that would further cut discretionary spending remained a possibility. Considerations of these circumstances led to the Budget Enforcement Act of 1990 (BEA), which created a "firewall" between discretionary spending and direct spending. Caps were set for discretionary spending and were enforced by sequestration that would make cuts solely to non-exempt discretionary spending programs. In addition, PAYGO was established to require that the net effect of new direct spending and revenue legislation did not increase the deficit (or reduce a surplus). PAYGO was enforced by a sequestration process that would make cuts solely to non-exempt direct spending programs.

S. 245 proposes to divide spending into three categories for the purpose of sequestration: direct spending, discretionary security spending, and discretionary non-security spending. S. 245 directs that each category receive a reduction "in proportion to the growth in outlays in such category from the previous fiscal year." Programs within each category would receive a uniform reduction commensurate with that category's overall growth.

The prospect that programs may remain vulnerable to automatic reductions in addition to those cuts that have already been made through legislative action might remove any incentive for Congress to enact reductions in spending for those programs in the first place. One proposal to address this potential difficulty could be to provide protection against sequestration for programs that have already been reduced through legislative action in the same year, either by exempting them from automatic cuts or limiting the amount of cuts.

Alternative Procedures

Proposals may include procedures for a congressional response to an automatic reduction order. Specifically, they may include expedited parliamentary procedures that would allow Congress to consider and pass legislation achieving the spending target in order to avoid an imminent automatic reduction. Expedited procedures, also referred to as "fast-track" procedures, are often included to ensure that specific legislation can be considered and voted on in a timely way and to protect it from procedural obstacles faced by most legislation.[32]

Under the Gramm-Rudman-Hollings Act, the President's initial sequestration order was due September 1, but would not take effect until the President's final sequestration order on October 15. This left Congress time to pass deficit reduction legislation of their choice to avoid sequestration. The act also provided expedited procedures for Senate consideration of such legislation. Specifically, it stated that such a measure "shall be considered in the Senate to be reconciliation bills or resolutions for the purposes of the Congressional Budget Act of 1974."[33]

S. 245 includes a section titled "Congressional Action," which provides that if an August 20 report from OMB projects a sequestration, the House and Senate Budget Committees "may report a resolution directing their committees to change the existing law to achieve the goals outlined in the August 20 report." It does not, however, include expedited procedures for the consideration of such spending reduction legislation.

H.R. 4529 (111th Congress) included a section titled "Alternate Spending Reduction Legislation in the House of Representatives," providing that after the OMB director issues a final sequestration order, but before the end of the session, the House or Senate majority leader may introduce a joint resolution that either directs the President to modify the most recent order or provides an alternative to eliminate the spending excess. H.R. 4529 went on to describe the expedited procedures under which this joint resolution can be considered. Some of these expedited procedures include discharging a House committee that has been referred the joint resolution, but has not yet reported it; placing the measure directly on the calendar in the Senate, as opposed to referring it to committee; limiting debate in the Senate to 10 hours; requiring amendments in the Senate to be germane; and limiting debate on each amendment to 30 minutes.

OBSERVATIONS FROM A HISTORICAL PERSPECTIVE

The purpose of overall limits on spending is to restrain, and in most cases, to reduce total spending. The inclusion in these proposals of both a spending limit and an automatic enforcement mechanism can be perceived as attempting to ensure that reductions in spending will actually occur. Examination of historical experience with mechanisms of this kind, however, may raise questions about the validity of the assumptions underlying this expectation. A closer examination of this experience may assist in determining how effective these mechanisms are likely to be. An accurate assessment of the implications of current proposals, however, requires attention to the specific means by which the various plans propose to bring about spending reductions.

One assumption that may lie behind some proposals for spending limits is that target levels of spending will ultimately be made, not through the application of the automatic enforcement mechanism, but through legislative action. This result would presumably require Congress and the President to negotiate an agreement on the spending reductions that are to be implemented through legislation. Proponents might expect that if a limit on total spending is in place, an agreement to reduce spending sufficiently to meet the statutory targets might result if any of three general conditions are met.

First, Congress and the President may come to an agreement based solely on a shared desire to reduce spending. If such a desire is present, however, then Congress and the President may be able to achieve the result without having to impose a prior statutory limit on themselves for the purpose.

Second, Congress and the President may come to an agreement because they wish, perhaps for political reasons, to adhere to the budgetary policy articulated in the spending limits. Although spending reductions would, under these circumstances, be related to the statutory spending limit, it is open to debate whether the existence of the limits would ensure such an agreement would be reached. Under present conditions, even in the absence of statutory limits, budgetary policies are already set out in the congressional budget resolution and the President's budget request, yet these are not always adhered to, often because of shifting priorities or unforeseen circumstances, such as a natural disaster or higher than projected direct spending levels.

Lastly, Congress and the President may reach agreement because the impact of the enforcement mechanism is so unattractive that it acts as a threat to force a negotiated compromise. Such a result seemed to be the intent behind the enforcement mechanism included in the Gramm-Rudman-Hollings Act, which threatened across-the-board spending cuts through sequestration if deficit targets were not met. Senator Phil Gramm, one of the chief sponsors of the act, stated that, "It was never the objective of Gramm-Rudman to trigger the sequester; the objective of Gramm-Rudman was to have the threat of the sequester force compromise and action."[34] In practice, however, it does not appear that in all cases this threat led to the anticipated result. Because legislation had not yet been enacted to reduce the deficit to required levels, sequestration was used for FY1986 and FY1990. This led many to believe that the sequester was not enough of a threat to force action. As a former staff member of the Senate Budget Committee stated at the time, "They thought they were creating something too awful to use. And it wound up being even easier."[35] Another former staffer stated, "I think the notion of sequester has lost its frightening characteristics. Sequestration was originally put in to push the nonsequester outcome. And if we've now gone through a few budget years where it's ho-hum, then there is no deterrence."[36]

On the other hand, situations also occurred in which, before the point arrived at which a sequestration would occur, the President and Congress successfully reached an agreement that cold be attributed to the desire to avoid sequestration. For example, in September of 1990, President George H.W. Bush and Congress reached a significant deficit reduction agreement that was subsequently implemented through annual appropriations bills and the Omnibus Budget Reconciliation Act of 1990 (P.L. 101-508). It could be argued that the willingness of President Bush to accept some revenue increases as part of this agreement, after having pledged in his campaign to reject tax increases, represented a response to the alternative of a sequester that would have reduced spending for non-exempt defense programs by 34.7% and non-exempt non-defense programs by 31.6%.

Nonetheless, these observations suggest that in some cases, Congress and the President may find it easier to allow an automatic budget enforcement mechanism to take effect rather than to negotiate an agreement. For one thing, Congress may find legislative inaction easier than action. In some cases, as well, allowing an automatic reduction may be politically easier than negotiating an agreement. In these respects, much may depend on how an automatic reduction is designed to work and which programs, if any, would be exempt. If proponents hope to promote a negotiated solution, they might wish to design the enforcement mechanism to be as unattractive as possible, so as to constitute a more severe threat. Yet it might be difficult to gather support for a proposal with a highly unattractive enforcement mechanism, because lawmakers, appreciating the difficulty of reaching a negotiated agreement, may fear that the enforcement mechanism will be used despite their best intention to reach such an agreement.

It can be argued that even if the threat of an automatic reduction does not force negotiation that reduces current spending, it may discourage spending on new programs. Some have said that the chief impact of Gramm-Rudman-Hollings was that it "acted as a brake on new initiatives," blocking, delaying, or reducing spending for new programs.[37]

Technical Compliance With, Setting Aside, and Revising Limits

Another assumption that may be made by proponents of statutory spending limits may be that compliance with statutory spending limits, either through legislative action or an automatic enforcement mechanism, will in fact result in spending reductions. Experience, however, shows that at least under some conditions, it may be possible to comply with the statutory requirements while still not achieving the intended reductions in actual spending.

If the statutory scheme provides exemptions from its requirements for "emergency spending," or for other specified programs, significant spending can occur that is not subject to the limits. For example, an exemption for spending labeled "emergency" was included in the Budget Enforcement Act of 1990. As displayed in Figure 1, levels of emergency spending increased in many years during the life of the act, growing to $47 billion in FY2002 ($18 billion in emergency defense spending and $29 billion in emergency non-defense spending).[38]

Furthermore, it may be possible to achieve compliance with statutory requirements through the use of various accounting devices that can discount the actual effects of spending. For example, the use of advance appropriations or directives to delay the incurring of obligations and the making of payments can permit spending to occur in ways that do not count against the established limits for a given fiscal year.[39]

If statutory spending limits are couched in terms of compliance with projections, it may become possible for enacted spending legislation to comply with the statutory limits even while actual spending turns out to exceed the target levels. This situation can arise because, as noted above, projections are highly sensitive to small changes in underlying assumptions and economic conditions. In addition, it may be possible, through the use of sufficiently optimistic assumptions, to adjust the applicable projected levels in ways that facilitate compliance with budgetary limits.

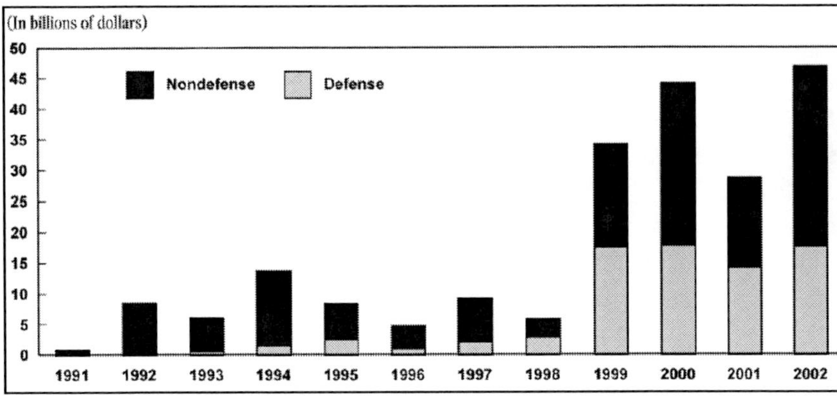

Source: Congressional Budget Office, *The Budget and Economic Outlook: Fiscal Years 2004-2013*, January 2003.

Notes: Excludes spending in 1991 and 1992 for Desert Storm and Desert Shield because that spending was offset by foreign contributions.

Figure 1. Emergency Budget Authority Under the Budget Enforcement Act of 1990.

Under Gramm-Rudman-Hollings, enacted spending legislation remained in technical compliance with the act, even though the deficit did not actually decline to the levels specified in the act. Former CBO Director, Robert D. Reischauer (1989-1995) stated that Gramm-Rudman-Hollings "encouraged reliance on overly optimistic economic and technical assumptions and transparent budget gimmickry."[40] Similarly, in a report to Congress and the President on compliance with the act, the comptroller general stated

> We report again, as we did last year, that compliance with the act does not necessarily result in meaningful deficit reduction. Over the last 4 years of technical compliance with the act, budgetary gimmicks have proliferated, adding billions of dollars in budget costs over the long run. There is also an aura of unreality about the budget projections made under provisions of the act. Over the years, OMB'S projections have sometimes been too optimistic. Additionally, the act limits OMB'S flexibility to correct its inaccurate estimates and technical mistakes. Such restrictions mean that the deficit estimate in this year's OMB reports cannot be taken as a meaningful projection of the deficit that will actually occur in fiscal year 1990.[41]

Advocacy of spending limits may rest on an assumption that as long as a future Congress does not repeal the limits enacted, it will adhere to them.

History suggests, however, that may not always be the case. Under both Gramm-Rudman-Hollings and the Budget Enforcement Act, Congress intervened several times to alter the existing process. In particular, when deficit targets were not being met under Gramm-Rudman-Hollings, Congress passed the Balanced Budget and Emergency Deficit Control Reaffirmation Act of 1987 (P.L. 100-119), which significantly revised the deficit targets upward and extended the period required to achieve a balanced budget. For example, the deficit target for FY1990, which had been $36 billion, was increased to $100 billion under the 1987 act.

Similarly, in several years in which deficit limits were expected to be breached, Congress passed legislation barring a sequester. For example, the Military Construction Appropriations Act for FY2001 (P.L. 106-246) was projected to breach the “other” category of the discretionary spending limits. To avoid sequestration, Congress included in the bill a provision barring a sequester.

In some years, moreover, Congress exempted new spending and revenue legislation from being counted against applicable limits. The Consolidated Appropriations Act for FY2000 (P.L. 106-113) included direct spending and revenue provisions that were projected to add $1.552 billion to the deficit for FY2000 and $15.193 billion for FY2000-FY2004. These budgetary effects, however, were exempted from being scored for purposes of PAYGO by a provision in the Appropriations Act.

Similarly, the Consolidated Appropriations Act for FY2001 (P.L. 106-554) included significant direct spending and revenue provisions by cross-reference. According to OMB’s final sequestration report, this measure, together with other measures, showed a net deficit increase of $10.52 billion for FY2001. A sequester was avoided, however, by a provision in the Consolidated Appropriations Act for FY2001 instructing the OMB director to reset the PAYGO balance for FY2001 to zero. This happened once again in the Defense Appropriations Act for FY2002 (P.L. 107-117), which instructed the OMB director to reset the balances of the PAYGO scorecard for FY2001 and FY2002 to zero. This removed $130.27 billion from counting under the budgetary enforcement mechanism, thereby preventing a PAYGO sequester.

It can be argued, nonetheless, that despite the potential for complications and for the use of budgetary devices that could be criticized as “gimmickry,” overall spending limits have the capacity to do much to reduce spending. For example, setting a national budgetary policy can focus considerable political and public attention on reducing spending. Further, regardless of the characteristics of a particular automatic reduction mechanism, if allowed to operate as prescribed, it *will* reduce spending, at least compared with current projected levels. As remarked by the former CBO director when discussing the success of a similar enforcement mechanism, Gramm-Rudman-Hollings, it "may not have brought the deficit cows back into the barn, but it has kept them from stampeding over the cliff."[42]

End Notes

[1] This report assumes some familiarity by the reader with the congressional budget process. For more information on the congressional budget process, see CRS Report RS20368, *Overview of the Congressional Budget Process*, by Bill Heniff Jr.

[2] This last term has been used by the Heritage Foundation. Brian Riedl, *10 Elements of Comprehensive Budget Process Reform*, The Heritage Foundation, June 15, 2006, http://www.heritage.org/research/reports/2006/06/10-elements-of-comprehensive-budget-process-reform?cfid=240494&cftoken=25e2923ef312de5c-212160d1-c63c-b796-be5768b8eceba165.

[3] Discretionary spending is provided annually through the appropriations process and is under the sole jurisdiction of the House and Senate Appropriations Committees. Direct spending is generally provided for in legislation outside of appropriations acts, and is under the jurisdiction of various authorizing committees.

[4] For example, H.J.Res. 1 and S.J.Res. 19 each include a cap on total outlays, but neither measure includes an enforcement mechanism. For more information, see CRS Report R41907, *A Balanced Budget Constitutional Amendment: Background and Congressional Options* , by James V. Saturno and Megan Suzanne Lynch.

[5] Legislative proposals were also introduced in the 111th Congress, such as H.R. 4529, introduced by Rep. Paul Ryan; and H.R. 5323, introduced by Rep. Lamar Smith.

[6] Congressional Budget Office, *The Budget and Economic Outlook FY2011-FY2021*, January 2011, pp.15, Table 1-4 available at http://www.cbo.gov/ftpdocs/120xx/doc12039/01-26_FY2011Outlook.pdf. For more information, see CRS Report R41685, *The Federal Budget: Issues for FY2011, FY2012, and Beyond*, by Mindy R. Levit.

[7] For more information, see CRS Report R41778, *Reducing the Budget Deficit: Policy Issues*, by Marc Labonte.

[8] The congressional budget resolution was established as a mechanism for coordinating congressional budgetary decision making between the House and Senate, by the Congressional Budget Act of 1974 (P.L. 93-344 as amended). The Budget Act requires that the budget resolution include specific components, several of which limit spending in some way. For more information, see CRS Report 98-815, *Budget Resolution Enforcement*, and CRS Report RS20368, *Overview of the Congressional Budget Process*, both by Bill Heniff Jr.

[9] Congress generally controls discretionary spending levels by enacting annual appropriations, whereas the funding for direct spending programs is typically controlled by laws other than appropriations (although they may be financed through appropriations actions). This means that the level of spending for most direct spending programs is determined each year with no congressional action or decision required, and it will continue until Congress takes some affirmative action to change the program itself. In FY2010, 40% of federal spending was discretionary spending and 55% was direct spending.

[10] Office of Management and Budget, *FY2012 Budget of the U.S. Government, Analytical Perspectives*, February 2011, p. 471.

[11] U.S. General Accounting Office, *Budget Policy, Issues in Capping Mandatory Spending*, 94-155, July 1994.

[12] Robert D. Reischauer, "Taxes and Spending Under Gramm-Rudman-Hollings," *National Tax Journal*, vol. 43, no. 3 (September 1990), p. 223.

[13] Ibid.

[14] Debt held by the public is different than total or gross debt because it doesn't include intergovernmental debt, which is debt issued for internal government transactions to trust funds and other federal accounts and not traded in capital markets. For more information, see CRS Report R41815, *Overview of the Federal Debt*, by D. Andrew Austin.

[15] For example, a White House press release stated, "Shared Sacrifice from All, Including the Most Fortunate Americans: The President believes strongly that, as we make difficult choices to live within our means, we cannot afford to make our deficit problem worse by extending the Bush tax cuts for the wealthiest Americans." "The President's framework would require ... A Debt Failsafe that will trigger across-the-board spending reductions (both in direct spending and spending through the tax code)" The White House, Office of the Press Secretary, "Fact Sheet: The President's Framework for Shared Prosperity and Shared Fiscal Responsibility," press release, April 13, 2011, http://www.whitehouse.gov/the-press-office/2011/04/13/fact-sheet-presidents-framework-shared-prosperity-and-shared-fiscal-resp.

[16] Oral and written testimony of Dr. Paul Van de Water, Senior Fellow, Center on Budget and Policy Priorities, before the Senate Finance Committee at the hearing on Budget Enforcement Mechanisms, May 4, 2011, accessible at http://finance.senate.gov/ hearings/hearing/?id=f47f0466-5056-a032-526c-15196aea18d1.

[17] Ibid.

[18] This quote is widely used when discussing various types of budget process reform, and it is typically attributed to former CBO Director Rudolph G. Penner. The first found reference is Elizabeth Wehr, "Congress Likely to Resist Budget Process Change," *Congressional Quarterly Weekly Report*, December 27, 1986, p. 3142.

[19] Associated Press, "Automatically triggered budget cuts have spotty record over past three decades," *Washington Post*, May 7, 2011. For more information regarding the Gramm-Rudman-Hollings Act, see CRS Report R41901, *Statutory Budget Controls in Effect Between 1985 and 2002*, by Megan Suzanne Lynch.

[20] Robert D. Reischauer, director, Congressional Budget Office, statement before the Subcommittee on Legislation and National Security, Committee on Government Operations, U.S. House of Representatives, May 13, 1993.

[21] Brian Riedl, *10 Elements of Comprehensive Budget Process Reform*, The Heritage Foundation, June 15, 2006, http://www.heritage.org/research/reports/2006/06/10-elements-of-comprehensive-budget-process-reform?cfid=240494&cftoken=25e2923ef312de5c-212160d1-c63c-b796-be5768b8eceba165.

[22] Edward P. Lazear, "How to Grow Out of the Deficit," *Wall Street Journal*, September 27, 2010.

[23] "The law should include a look-back sequester which corrects for deficit overages when the actual deficit spending totals for the year are calculated. This would allow for mid-course corrections to keep the nation on a deficit reduction glide-path before the deficit targets become unachievable." Oral and written testimony of the Honorable Phil Gramm (former Member of the House of Representatives 1979-1985 and U.S. Senator 1985-2002), before the Senate Finance Committee at the hearing on Budget Enforcement Mechanisms, May 4, 2011, accessible at http://finance.senate.gov/ hearings/hearing/?id=f47f0466-5056-a032-526c-15196aea18d1.

[24] A special rule is a simple resolution reported from the House Rules Committee, typically intended to regulate floor consideration of a specific legislative measure.

[25] P.L. 99-177. For further information see, CRS Report R41901, *Statutory Budget Controls in Effect Between 1985 and 2002*, by Megan Suzanne Lynch.

[26] If real economic growth was projected to be negative in two consecutive quarters, or if the Commerce Department reported that actual real growth was below 1% in two consecutive quarters, the deficit level provisions could be suspended.

[27] Within Statutory PAYGO, budgetary effects of new enacted direct spending and revenue provisions are recorded on two separate scorecards. At the end of a congressional session, the scorecards are evaluated to determine if a debit has been recorded for the current budget year; that is, if new legislation has increased or created a deficit. If no such debit is found, no action occurs. If a debit is found, however, the President must issue a sequestration order which automatically implements across-the-board cuts to non-exempt direct spending programs to compensate for the amount of the debit. For more information, see CRS Report R41157, *The Statutory Pay-As-You-Go Act of 2010: Summary and Legislative History*, by Bill Heniff Jr.

[28] Although not a traditional enforcement mechanism, the budget reconciliation process can also be used to enforce the levels included in the budget resolution, particularly for spending resulting from already enacted legislation. It is an optional, congressional process used to assist Congress in achieving the levels set forth in the budget resolution by instructing specific committees to report legislative changes within their jurisdiction that would achieve a certain budgetary goal. Once the specified committees develop legislation in response to the directive, the reported legislation is considered under expedited procedures in both the House and Senate CRS Report RL33030, *The Budget Reconciliation Process: House and Senate Procedures*, by Robert Keith and Bill Heniff Jr.

[29] P.L. 101-508.

[30] P.L. 105-33.

[31] Oral and written testimony before the Senate Finance Committee at the hearing on Budget Enforcement Mechanisms, May 4, 2011, accessible at http://finance.senate. gov/ hearings/hearing/?id=f47f0466-5056-a032-526c-15196aea18d1.

[32] For more information on expedited procedures, see CRS Report RS20234, *Expedited or "Fast-Track" Legislative Procedures*, by Christopher M. Davis.

[33] Section 254(c).

[34] Oral and written testimony of the Honorable Phil Gramm (former Member of the House of Representatives from 1979-1985 and U.S. Senator from 1985-2002), before the Senate Finance Committee at the hearing on Budget Enforcement Mechanisms, May 4, 2011, accessible at http://finance.senate.gov/hearings/hearing/?id=f47f0466-5056-a032-526c-15196aea18d1.

[35] Quote by Nell Payne, former Republican chief counsel to the Senate Budget Committee, as included in Lawrence J. Haas, "Losing Its Punch," *National Journal*, December 30, 1989, p. 3106.

[36] Quote by Steven I. Hoffman, a former House Republican leadership aide. Ibid.

[37] Robert D. Reischauer, "Taxes and Spending Under Gramm-Rudman-Hollings," *National Tax Journal*, vol. 43, no. 3 (September 1990), p. 228.

[38] Congressional Budget Office, *The Budget and Economic Outlook: Fiscal Years 2004-2013*, January 2003.

[39] Advance appropriations means that budget authority will become available one or more fiscal years after the fiscal year covered by the act. For more information, see CRS Report RS20441, *Advance Appropriations, Forward Funding, and Advance Funding*, by Sandy Streeter.

[40] Robert D. Reischauer, "Taxes and Spending Under Gramm-Rudman-Hollings," *National Tax Journal*, vol. 43, no. 3 (September 1990), p. 223.

[41] U.S. General Accounting Office, *Deficit Reductions for Fiscal Year 1990, Compliance with the Balanced Budget and Emergency Deficit Control Act of 1985*, GAO-AFMD-90-40, November 1989, p. 1.

[42] Reischauer, "Taxes and Spending Under Gramm-Rudman-Hollings," p. 232.

INDEX

J

K

L

M

N

O

P

R